Adventures with Digital Electronics

TOM DUNCAN

JOHN MURRAY

Other books in the Adventure series

Electronics
Microelectronics
Physics

Acknowledgements

Thanks are due to Brian Openshaw for the care with which he read the manuscript, to Freda for typing it, to Howard Jay for several useful suggestions and to my former students, especially Stephen Rochford, Robert Till and Nicholas Williams, for developing some of the projects.

© Tom Duncan 1982

First published 1982
Reprinted 1985

John Murray (Publishers) Ltd
50 Albemarle Street, London W1X 4BD

All rights reserved. Unauthorised
duplication contravenes existing laws.

Printed in Great Britain by
Fletcher & Son Ltd, Norwich

British Library Cataloguing in Publication Data

Duncan, Tom
   Adventures with digital electronics
   1. Microprocessors
   1. Title
   621.3819′5835   TK7895.M5

  ISBN 0–7195–3943–9
  ISBN 0–7195–3875–0 Pbk

Contents

How to start   4
About digital electronics   5
Logic gates   7
Multivibrators   9
Flip-flops   11
Counters   14
Shift registers   16
Memories   17
Arithmetic circuits   18
Code converters   21
Displays   23
Building circuits   24

PROJECTS

1 Electronic shooting gallery   28
2 Quiz-game switches   32
3 Two-way traffic lights I   36
4 Two-way traffic lights II   40
5 Pedestrian crossing signals   44
6 Electronic fruit machine   48
7 Computer space invaders   52
8 Electronic adder   58

Parts lists   63
Addresses   64

How to start

The first part of the book (pages 5 to 27) deals with the different kinds of digital integrated circuits, commonly called ICs or 'chips', and other components that are used in the second part for the projects. By studying the first part before, while and/or after you tackle a project you will get a better understanding of what some of the basic building blocks of digital electronics do. The circuits for the projects will also make more sense.

You might even be tempted to have a go at designing your own circuit before scrutinizing the one given. Usually there is more than one way of putting together an electronic system to do a certain job.

Information is given on page 64 about how to obtain a kit for *Adventures with Digital Electronics*. Guidance is also given about obtaining the components separately, should you prefer to do that.

Construction in each project is on *two* standard circuit boards (no soldering required) and a 9 V battery acts as the power supply in all cases. You will also need a pair of blunt-nosed pliers, a small screwdriver and either a pair of side-cutting pliers or wire strippers. In addition, a magnifying glass is a help for checking circuits.

MAY ALL YOUR SYSTEMS GO!

About digital electronics

Electronic circuits can be classified broadly as being either *digital* or *analogue* (also called linear). In the first type, transistors (discrete or in ICs) act as switches; in the second type they usually act as amplifiers.

(a) Digital circuits Digital circuits are used in computers, calculators, electronic watches, factory robots, television games and increasingly in domestic appliances like washing machines. They are *two-state* devices designed so that their output and input voltages are either 'high', i.e. near the supply voltage, or 'low' (e.g. near 0 V) and also so that they switch very rapidly from one state to the other.

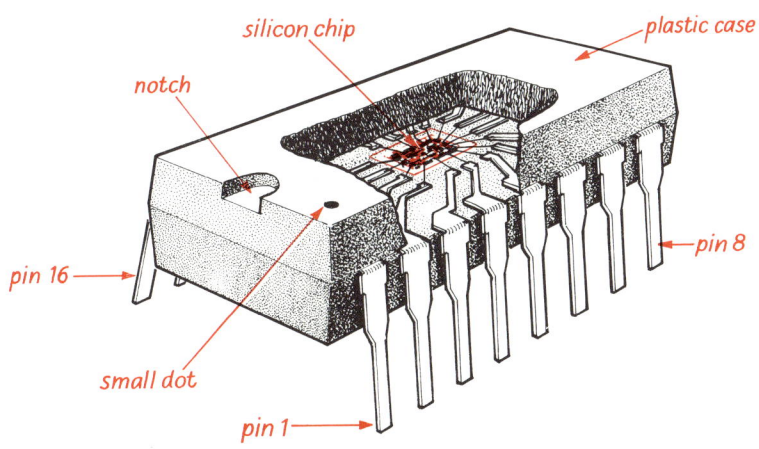

Today, digital circuits are produced as ICs with all (or most) of the components (transistors and perhaps diodes, resistors and capacitors) made at the same time and connected together on a tiny 'chip' of silicon about 5 mm square and 0.5 mm thick. The chip is enclosed in a plastic case with the connecting pins, spaced 0.1 inch apart, usually arranged in two lines on either side. In this dual-in-line (d.i.l.) arrangement, pin 1 is identified by a 'notch' or a 'small dot' at one end of the top of the case.

(b) CMOS and TTL There are two main families of digital circuits. One, called CMOS (pronounced 'see-moss' and standing for Complementary Metal Oxide Semiconductor), uses field effect transistors (known as 'fets'). The other, TTL (standing for Transistor-Transistor-Logic), uses the junction or bipolar transistor (known as 'the' transistor).

We will be using some of the 4000B series of CMOS chips (with one exception – the 556 timer, page 9) for several reasons. First, they work off any voltage between 3 V and 15 V, which need not be stabilized. Second, they take very small currents under the conditions in the projects. Third, they are highly immune to 'noise', i.e. they can withstand relatively large unwanted stray voltages (such as may arise when a connection is made or broken) without a false change of their output state. These features enable them to be operated satisfactorily from a 9 V battery; their 'high' state is then near 9 V and their 'low' state near 0 V.

(c) Precautions with CMOS Static electric charges can build up on the input pins (due to the very high input impedance of CMOS chips) when, for example, they touch insulating materials (e.g. plastics, clothes) in warm, dry conditions. Damage can then occur. CMOS chips are therefore supplied either in antistatic or conductive carriers. Also, protective circuits are incorporated at the inputs which operate when the IC is connected to the power supply.

Here are *three rules* you should follow.

1 Keep the IC in the carrier in which it is supplied until it is inserted in the circuit.

2 Connect all *unused inputs* to either the positive or the negative terminal of the battery, depending on the circuit. (This is done in all the circuits given.)

3 Check very carefully before switching on a circuit that the *battery is correctly connected to the IC*, i.e. V_{DD} (pin 16 or 14) to the battery positive and V_{SS} (pin 8 or 7) to battery negative. (In these symbols D and S refer to the drain and source respectively of the fets in the IC.)

Logic gates

Logic gates are switching circuits in which the state of the output at any instant depends on the present states of all the inputs (usually there is more than one). They 'open' and give a 'high' output only for certain input combinations.

There are several types, the behaviour of each type is described by a *truth table* showing what the output is for all possible inputs. In the table, the 'high' and 'low' states, i.e. near 9 V or near 0 V, are represented by 1 and 0 respectively and are referred to as logic levels 1 and 0. In practice the 'high' and 'low' states can be detected readily using a light-emitting diode (LED) as explained later (page 23).

(a) NOT gate or inverter This is the simplest gate, it has one input and one output. It produces a 'high' output if the input is 'low', i.e. *not* 'high', and vice-versa. The symbol most often used for it and the truth table are shown here.

Input	Output
0	1
1	0

(b) NAND, AND, NOR and OR gates All these have two or more inputs and one output. The truth tables and symbols for 2-input gates are shown below.

NAND

Inputs		Output
A	B	C
0	0	1
0	1	1
1	0	1
1	1	0

AND

Inputs		Output
A	B	C
0	0	0
0	1	0
1	0	0
1	1	1

NOR

Inputs		Output
A	B	C
0	0	1
0	1	0
1	0	0
1	1	0

OR

Inputs		Output
A	B	C
0	0	0
0	1	1
1	0	1
1	1	1

Try to remember the following properties of the different gates.

NAND : output is 1 unless all inputs are 1
AND : output is 1 only when all inputs are 1
NOR : output is 1 only when all inputs are 0
OR   : output is 1 unless all inputs are 0

(c) Exclusive OR gate It has only two inputs and gives a 1 output when either input is 1 but not when both are 1. Unlike the ordinary OR gate (sometimes called the *inclusive* OR gate) it excludes the case of both inputs being 1 for an output of 1.

It is also called the *difference* gate because the output is 1 when the inputs are different.

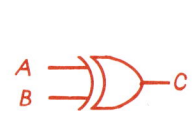

Inputs		Output
A	B	C
0	0	0
0	1	1
1	0	1
1	1	0

(d) Combining NAND gates A useful property of NAND (and NOR) gates is that they can be combined to make any of the other logic gates. The arrangements are given below. You can check that each one gives the correct output for the various input combinations by constructing a stage-by-stage truth table, as has been done for the NOR gate made from four NAND gates.

Note that if all the inputs on a NAND (or NOR) gate are joined together to form one input, we get a NOT gate or inverter.

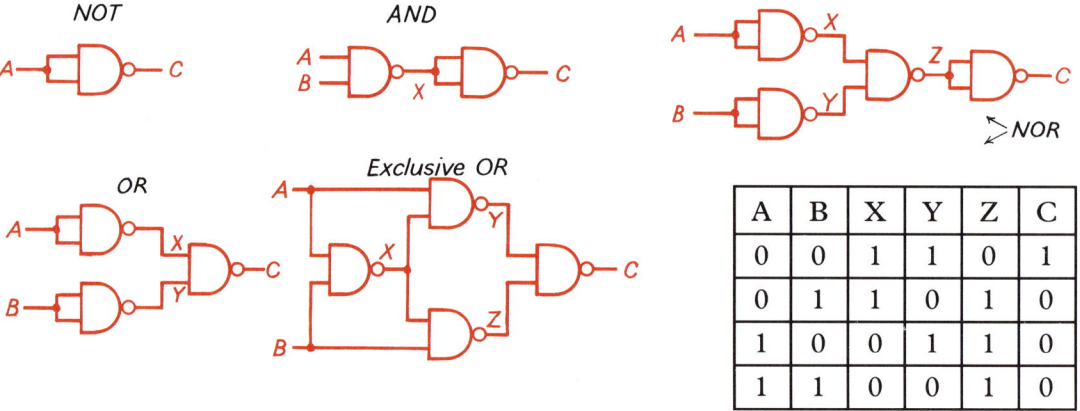

(e) Some useful logic gate ICs Logic gate IC packages usually have several gates on the same chip with common power supply connections. Those shown below are used in the projects. V_{DD} and V_{SS} go to supply + and − respectively.

4001B is a quad 2-input NOR gate, with four identical two-input NOR gates.
4002B is a dual 4-input NOR gate, i.e. there are two NOR gates with four inputs per gate. NC indicates no connection to pins 6 and 8.
4011B is a quad 2-input NAND gate.

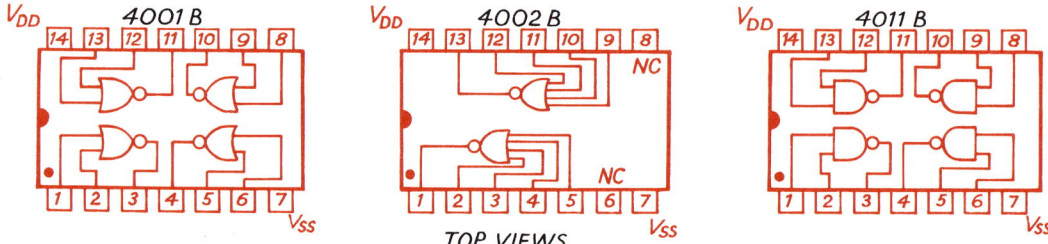

TOP VIEWS

Multivibrators

There are three types; two are considered here. In an *astable* or 'free-running' multivibrator, the output switches automatically to and fro from the 'high' to the 'low' state to give a continuous stream of 'square' voltage pulses, i.e. it is a square-wave generator. It is not stable in either state (hence 'astable') and, among other things, is used to supply 'clock' or 'trigger' pulses to synchronize (i.e. keep in step) the various parts of digital systems.

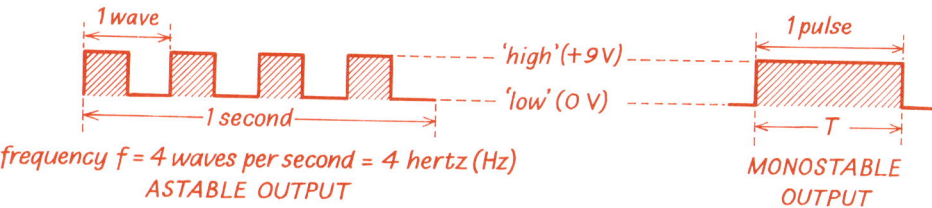

A *monostable* or 'one-shot' multivibrator is stable in its 'low' state and when suitably 'triggered' by an incoming signal its output voltage switches to the unstable 'high' state for a certain time before returning to the 'low' state, where it remains until triggered again. It produces one 'square' output pulse.

(a) 556 astable/monostable Known popularly as a 'timer', this IC contains two separate multivibrators; each can be used either as an astable or as a monostable. It can drive a loudspeaker directly, its maximum output current being 200 mA. As an astable it needs two external resistors ($R1$ and $R2$) and one capacitor ($C1$). As a monostable, one external resistor ($R3$) and capacitor ($C3$) are essential. The circuit below shows how one 'half' of the IC (pins 1 to 6) is connected as an astable and how the other 'half' (pins 8 to 13) can operate as a monostable.

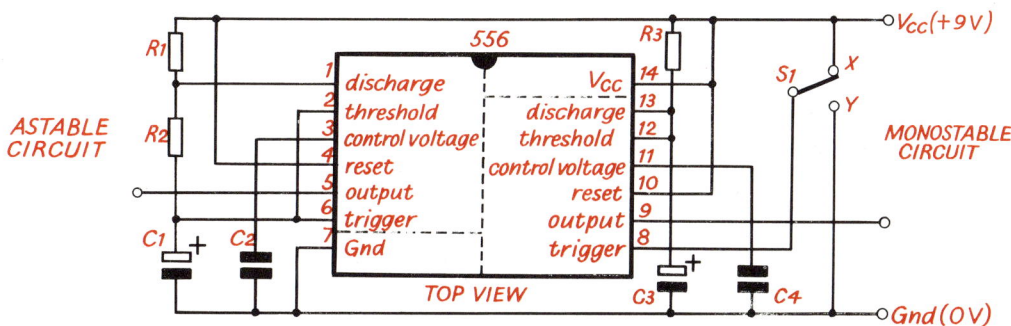

The frequency f of the square waves from the astable is given by

$$f = \frac{1.4}{(R1 + 2 \times R2)C1} \text{ Hz},$$

where $R1$ and $R2$ are in ohms (Ω) and $C1$ is in farads (F).
If $R2 \gg R1$, then

$$f = \frac{1.4}{2 \times R2 \times C1} = \frac{0.7}{R2 \times C1} \text{ Hz}.$$

For example, if $R1 = 10\,\text{k}\Omega$, $R2 = 1\,\text{M}\Omega = 10^6\,\Omega$ and $C1 = 1\,\mu\text{F} = 10^{-6}\,\text{F}$, then $f = 0.7/(10^6 \times 10^{-6}) = 0.7\,\text{Hz}$.

Two useful features of the 556 as an astable are, (*i*) if the voltage on 'reset' is less than 0.7 V or so, it stops working, and (*ii*) f can be changed independently of $R1$, $R2$ and $C1$ by applying a voltage (e.g. 4.5 V) to 'control voltage' (which normally goes to 0 V via a 0.01 μF capacitor $C2$), i.e. *frequency modulation* occurs.

The time T of the pulse from the monostable is given by

$$T = 1.1 \times R3 \times C3.$$

If $R3 = 2.2\,\text{M}\Omega = 2.2 \times 10^6\,\Omega$ and $C3 = 1\,\mu\text{F} = 10^{-6}\,\text{F}$, then $T = 1.1 \times 2.2 \times 10^6 \times 10^{-6} = 2.4\,\text{s}$. The monostable is triggered by the falling (negative-going) edge (⌐) of a pulse applied to 'trigger', obtained for example, by rapidly switching $S1$ from X to Y and back to X again so that the triggering time is less than the output pulse time T.

(b) 4047B astable/monostable

This IC has a much lower power output than the 556 but it needs only one external capacitor (C, not an electrolytic) and one resistor (R) and has three astable outputs – called Q, $\bar{Q}$ (pronounced 'not Q') and 'oscillator'. Q and $\bar{Q}$ are complements, i.e. one is 'high' when the other is 'low'. Their frequency f_1 is given by

$$f_1 = \frac{0.23}{R \times C} \text{ Hz}.$$

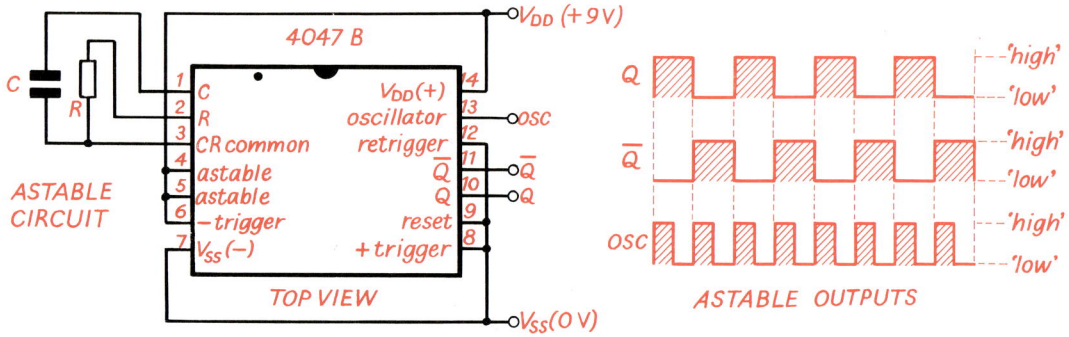

If $R = 2.2\,\text{M}\Omega = 2.2 \times 10^6\,\Omega$ and $C = 0.1\,\mu\text{F} = 10^{-7}\,\text{F}$, then $f_1 = 0.23/(2.2 \times 10^6 \times 10^{-7}) = 1\,\text{Hz}$. The frequency f_2 of the oscillator output is $2f_1 = 2\,\text{Hz}$ in this case. The astable circuit (shown above) works, i.e. is enabled, only if the voltage on 'astable' (pin 5) does not fall below about $\frac{1}{2}V_{DD}$ (i.e. 4.5 V if $V_{DD} = 9\,\text{V}$).

The connections for triggering the IC as a monostable are given in the table. Both rising and falling edges can be used. The pulse time $T = 2.5\,RC$, R and C being connected as in the astable circuit.

Trigger	Pin connections		Input trigger to	Output pulse from
	to V_{DD}	to V_{SS}		
rising edge	4, 14	5, 6, 7, 9, 12	8	10, 11
falling edge	4, 8, 14	5, 7, 9, 12	6	10, 11

Facilities we will not require are provided by 'astable' (pin 4) in astable operation and by 'retrigger' (pin 12) and 'reset' (pin 9) in monostable operation.

Flip-flops

A flip-flop or bistable multivibrator is stable in both the 'high' and the 'low' output states, i.e. its output, Q, can be 1 or 0 indefinitely. To make it change, i.e. flip to the 'high' state or flop to the 'low' state, an appropriate input pulse is required. Basically it is a store or memory circuit, much used in counters (page 14), shift registers (page 16) and memories (page 17). Symbols for the different types of flip-flop are shown; note that the complementary outputs, $\bar{Q}$, are also available.

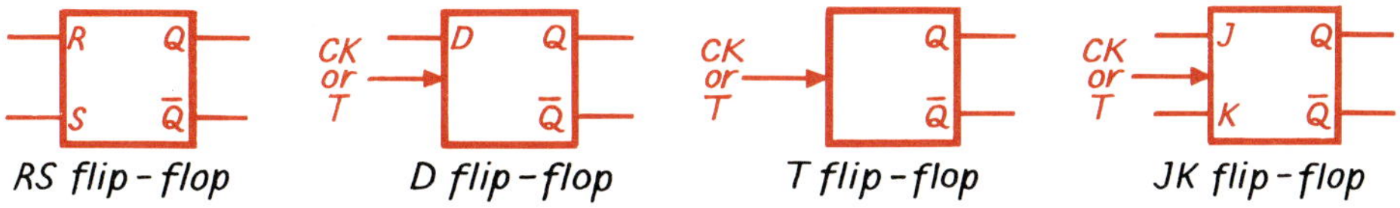

RS flip-flop   D flip-flop   T flip-flop   JK flip-flop

Two versions of the D flip-flop, so named because of its *data* (D) input, will be described.

(a) 4013B dual D flip-flop This IC consists of two independent D flip-flops with common power supply pins. There are three ways of operation.

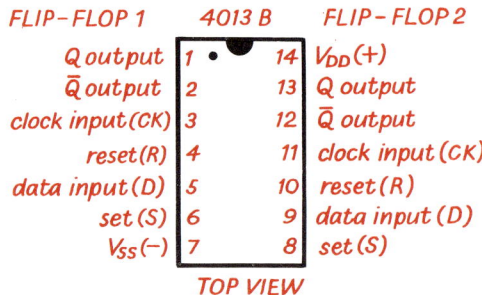

DIRECT MODE

Inputs		Outputs	
R	S	Q	Q̄
1	0	0	1
0	1	1	0
1	1	see text	
0	0		

CLOCKED MODE

Inputs		Outputs	
CK	D	Q	Q̄
⌐	0	0	1
⌐	0	0	1
⌐	1	1	0
⌐	1	1	0

In the *direct mode* it behaves as an RS type. If R is 'high' and S 'low', it *resets* with Q 'low' and Q̄ 'high'. If R = 0 and S = 1, it switches to its other stable state in which it is *set* with Q = 1 and Q̄ = 0. If R = 1 and S = 1, it means we are trying to get Q (and Q̄) to be 1 and 0 at the same time, which is not sense, and so this input condition is avoided.

In the *clocked* (or triggered) *mode*, R and S must be 0. When a rising (positive-going ⌐) pulse is applied to CK (or T), if D = 0, clocking makes Q = 0 and Q̄ = 1 and both outputs retain these states until the next clock pulse arrives (even if D becomes 1 or the clock pulse falls ⌐). When D = 1, clocking makes Q = 1 and Q̄ = 0. To sum up, in D-type action, *the state (1 or 0) of the D input is transferred to the Q output during the rising edge of a clock pulse* and not before. The direct inputs R and S override the clock input.

In the *toggling mode*, the flip-flop changes its output state on successive clock pulses and behaves like a T flip-flop. To make this occur D is connected to Q̄ as shown on p. 13 and when the first clock pulse is applied (e.g. by switching *S*1 from X to Y to X), Q changes its state, say from 'low' to 'high' (AB) on the rising edge *ab* of the clock pulse. On the rising edge *cd* of the second clock pulse, Q changes again, this time from 'high' to 'low' (DC). Q goes 'high' again (EF) on the rising edge *ef* of the third clock pulse and so on. The graphs of clock input and Q show that Q goes 'high' once every two clock pulses. That is, the frequency of the output pulses from Q is *half* that of the clock pulses. A toggling flip-flop is therefore a *divide-by-two* circuit.

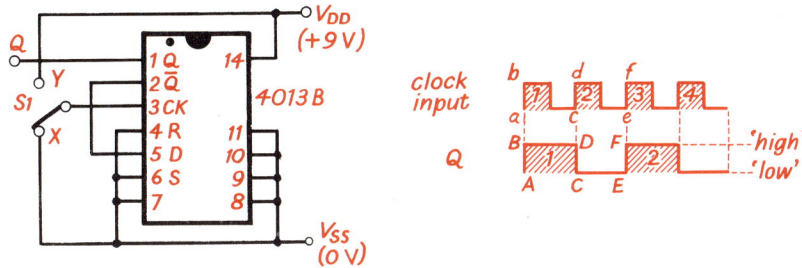

Toggling occurs because when Q = 1, Q̄ = 0 = D and so on the rising edge of the next clock pulse, the D level is transferred to Q, i.e. Q becomes 0 while Q̄ and D become 1 and so on.

In Project 5 (*Pedestrian crossing signals*) the 4013B is used in both direct and clocked modes and in Project 3 (*Traffic lights I*) it toggles.

(b) 4042B quad D latch   Four identical D flip-flops are enclosed in the same IC package with a common clock input (CK). Each flip-flop has its own D input, Q and Q̄ outputs. *As soon as* a D input is applied, in this case it is transferred to the corresponding Q output provided CK and POL are in the same state, i.e. either both 'high' or both 'low'. If the state of CK is then changed so that it is *different* from that of POL, the 'high' or 'low' state of each Q (and Q̄) output is stored or 'latched'. A subsequent change at any of the D inputs does not affect the Q (or Q̄) outputs – so long as CK and POL are still different.

	Inputs		Outputs	
CK	POL	D	Q	Q̄
0	0	0	0	1
0	0	1	1	0
1	0	0/1	latches	
1	1	0	0	1
1	1	1	1	0
0	1	0/1	latches	

The Q̄₁, Q̄₂, Q̄₃ and Q̄₄ outputs are always the complements of Q₁, Q₂, Q₃ and Q₄ respectively.

Unlike the 4013B which is *edge-triggered*, the 4042B is *level-controlled* by the clock input. Also its four stages cannot be joined in series (cascade). Its action is well illustrated in Project 2 (*Quiz-game switches*).

13

Counters

An electronic counter counts the number of pulses entering its 'clock' (or 'trigger') input. It consists of several flip-flops connected so that they can toggle (p. 12). Counting is done in binary code, the 'high' and 'low' states representing the binary digits (bits) 1 and 0 respectively.

In a *ripple* or *asynchronous* counter the output (Q) of one flip-flop feeds the clock input (CK) of the next. This type is satisfactory only for small counts, being slower (because each flip-flop has to wait for a clock pulse from the one before) than the more reliable but more complex *synchronous* counter in which all flip-flops are clocked simultaneously. The block diagram for an asynchronous counter is shown below using D flip-flops (with D joined to $\bar{Q}$ to give toggling); it can handle four bits, Q_4 giving the most significant one.

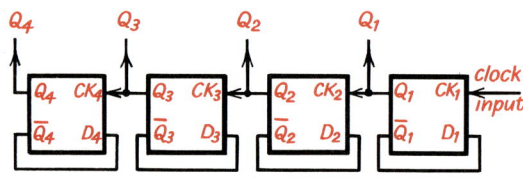

FOUR-BIT RIPPLE COUNTER

Details follow of three popular synchronous counter ICs.

(a) 4516B binary counter This is a four-bit counter whose four outputs represent counts of $Q_1 = 1$, $Q_2 = 2$, $Q_3 = 4$ and $Q_4 = 8$. When the count is, say, 3, Q_1 and Q_2 are 'high'. The maximum count is 1111 in binary (=15) and is obtained when all four outputs are 'high' (see timing diagram).

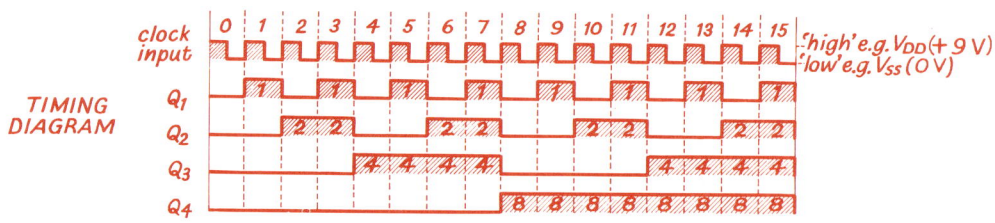

On the rising edge (⎍) of a clock pulse the count increases by one if U/D is 'high' and decreases by one if it is 'low'. Normally R, CI and PE are kept 'low'. If R is taken 'high', the counter resets to zero. Taking CI 'high' stops the count and this input may be used to prevent (inhibit) or allow (enable) counting. If PE is made 'high' the counter reads the total count on the four preset inputs (which are weighted $P_1 = 1$, $P_2 = 2$, $P_3 = 4$ and $P_4 = 8$) regardless of the clock input. The truth table sums up the behaviour of the counter.

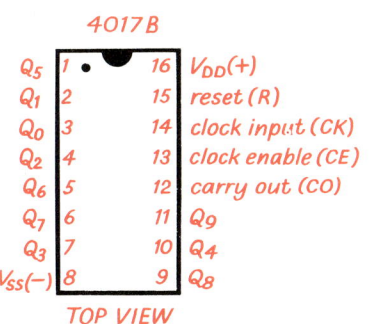

CK	R	CI	PE	U/D	Action
⌐	0	0	0	1	counts up
⌐	0	0	0	0	counts down
X	1	X	X	X	resets to zero
X	0	1	0	X	no count
X	0	X	1	X	counts presets

X = does not matter if 'high' or 'low'
⌐ = rising edge of a clock pulse

For counts above 15, two or more counters can be joined in ripple mode if CO of the first feeds CK of the second and so on. Alternatively if CO of one is taken to CI of the next they are in synchronous mode.

In Project 4 (*Two-way traffic lights II*) three outputs of the 4516B are used to control an eight-stage sequence of operations.

(b) 4510B BCD counter The pin connections are the same as on the 4516B and the behaviour is similar except that it uses only ten of the sixteen possible output combinations. The maximum count is 9 (i.e. Q_1 and Q_4 'high') and the decimal numbers 0 to 9 are represented at the four outputs in binary code – hence binary coded decimal (BCD).

When used with a suitable decoder (page 22) it shows the count more conveniently in decimal form on a 7-segment LED display (page 23).

(c) 4017B decade counter This has ten outputs (Q_0 to Q_9) and each goes 'high' in turn on the rising edge of successive clock pulses (see timing diagram) provided that R and CE are both 'low'.

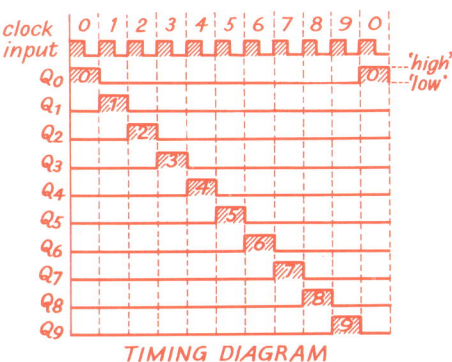

When R is taken 'high', the counter resets to zero and in this condition Q_0 is 'high' and all other outputs are 'low'. R must be returned to 'low' for counting to start again. Counting stops if CE is made 'high' at any time.

Most of the facilities of this counter are used in Project 1 (*Electronic shooting gallery*).

15

Shift registers

A shift register stores a binary number and shifts it out when required. It consists of several flip-flops, one for each bit (0 or 1) in the number. The bits may be fed in and out serially, i.e. one after the other, or in parallel, i.e. all together. Shift registers are used in calculators to store two binary numbers before they are added (see Project 8 – *Electronic adder*).

(a) Types In the four-bit *serial-input-serial-output* (SISO) type shown below, D flip-flops are used and the Q output of each one is applied to the D input of the next. Each bit enters the register from the left and moves one flip-flop to the right every clock pulse. Four pulses are needed to enter a four-bit number (e.g. 0101 = 5) and another four to move it out.

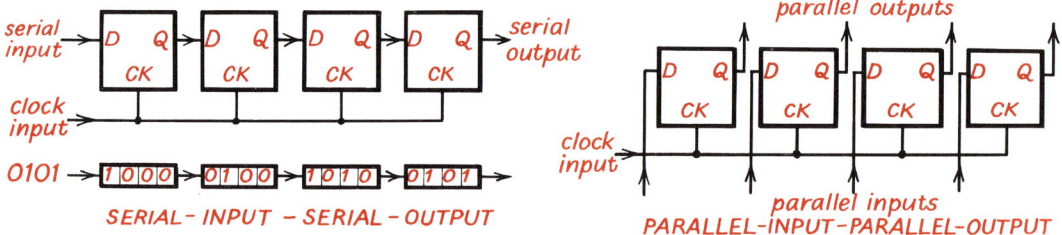

In the *parallel-input-parallel-output* (PIPO) type all bits enter their D inputs simultaneously and are transferred together to their Q outputs (where they are stored) by the same clock pulse. They can then be shifted out in parallel.

Two other arrangements are serial-input-parallel-output (SIPO) and parallel-input-serial-output (PISO).

(b) 4035B four-bit universal shift register Shifting in this versatile register occurs on the rising edge of a clock pulse.

To *serial-load* bits, P/S and R are held 'low' and T/C is made 'high'. The J and K inputs (which belong to a JK flip-flop that controls the input to the four D-types that follow) are joined together to form the serial input.

To *parallel-load* bits, R is kept 'low' while T/C and P/S are held 'high' and the bits are applied to inputs $A_4A_3A_2A_1$, the least significant bit (lsb) to A_1. On the next clock pulse the number is stored in the register and is available at the four Q outputs either as a parallel output, or if P/S is made 'low', for shifting out serially.

Making R 'high' puts all outputs in their 'low' state whether the register is in series or parallel mode. If T/C is made 'low', all outputs give the complement $\bar{Q}$ of what is stored in the register, i.e. 0 for 1 and vice versa.

Memories

A memory stores in binary code the *data*, i.e. information and instructions required by an electronic system such as a computer. One type, called the *random access memory* (RAM) consists, in one form, of an array of a large number of flip-flops each storing one bit (0 or 1). The array is arranged so that the bits are in groups, known as 'words' of, for example, four bits each.

Every 'word' has its own location or *address* in the memory which is identified by a certain binary number. In a RAM, access is gained in a random way, i.e. they can be 'read' in any order and it is not necessary to start at the first address and go through each in turn until the wanted 'word' is reached. 'Reading' a word does not destroy it; alternatively, we can 'write' a new 'word' into any address. RAMs are said to be 'volatile' because the data written in is lost almost as soon as the power supply to the RAM is switched off.

(a) Memory organization The table below shows the organization and part of the contents of a memory having 16 addresses each storing a four-bit word.

Address					Data				
Decimal	Binary				Binary				Decimal
	msb			lsb	msb			lsb	
0	0	0	0	0	0	1	0	1	5
1	0	0	0	1	1	1	0	0	12
⋮	⋮	⋮	⋮	⋮	⋮	⋮	⋮	⋮	⋮
14	1	1	1	0	0	0	1	1	3
15	1	1	1	1	0	1	1	1	7

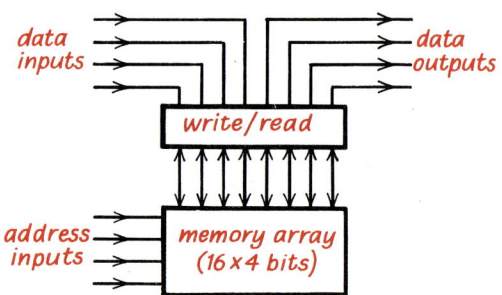

For example, in the location with *address* 1110 (= 14), the *data* stored is the four-bit word 0011 (= 3). This kind of organization needs four address inputs to select a location (since four bits give any of the sixteen decimal numbers 0 and 15). Four data inputs and outputs are also necessary to enable a four-bit 'word' to be 'written' in or to let one be 'read' out – as shown on the block diagram on the left.

(b) 40114B 16-word 4-bit RAM The least significant bits (lsb) are handled by address input A, data input 1 and data output 1 and the most significant bits (msb) by address input D, data input and output 4.

To 'write' data in, ME and WE must both be 'low'.

To 'read' the data in a selected address, ME should be 'low' and WE 'high'. The *complement* of the 'word' then appears at the data outputs. The *true* 'word' can be obtained at the data outputs if, when the word is 'written' in, it is first inverted by having an inverter (page 7) in each data input line – as is done in Project 7 (*Computer space invaders*).

Arithmetic circuits

Electronic arithmetic uses only the two bits 0 and 1 of the binary code. Two kinds of circuit required are *adders* and *magnitude comparators*.

(a) Adders A *half-adder* adds *two bits* at a time. The four cases it has to deal with are listed in the table at the top of the next page; A and B represent the bits to be added. Note that 1 + 1 has a sum of 0 and a carry of 1.

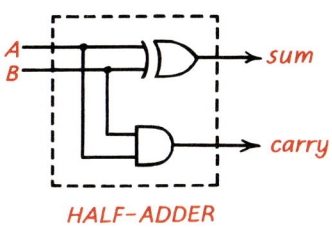

HALF-ADDER

| Inputs || Outputs ||
A	B	Sum	Carry
0	0	0	0
0	1	1	0
1	0	1	0
1	1	0	1

The half-adder circuit shown uses an exclusive OR gate and an AND gate (page 7); one output gives the *sum* of the two bits and the other gives the *carry*. Check that the circuit does give the required outputs by applying the properties of the two gates to the various input combinations.

A *full-adder* adds *three bits* at a time, a necessary operation when two multi-bit binary numbers are added. In the example right, 3 (11 in binary) is added to 3, i.e. two two-bit numbers are added. In the least significant (right-hand) column we have 1 + 1 = sum 0 and carry 1. In the middle column three bits have to be added because of the carry from the first one. The answer for this column is 1 + 1 + 1 = sum 1 and carry 1. A full-adder is used for each column and needs therefore *three* inputs A, B, C (one from the carry bit from a previous addition) and *two* outputs, one for the sum and one for the carry. Check that the circuit given below produces the outputs shown in the table beside it for three-bit addition of the different input combinations.

```
    4 2 1
    1 1   = 3
  + 1 1   = 3
  1 1 0   = 6
```

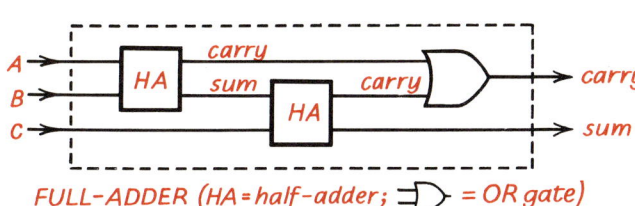

FULL-ADDER (HA = half-adder; ⊃= OR gate)

| Inputs ||| Outputs ||
A	B	C	Sum	Carry
0	0	1	1	0
0	1	1	0	1
1	1	1	1	1

To add 3 + 3 electronically (i.e. 11 + 11 in binary), two full-adders in parallel are required, as shown (although the first, FA_1, need only be a half-adder since it handles just two bits).

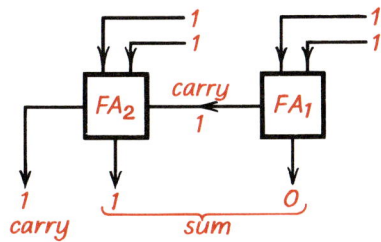

19

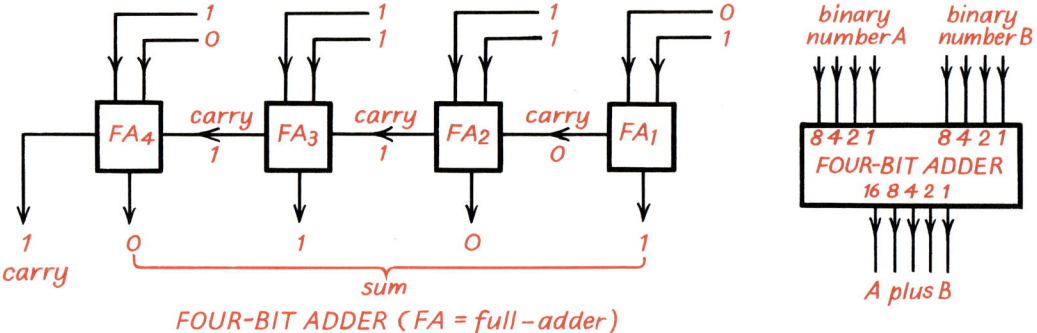

FOUR-BIT ADDER (FA = full-adder)

To add two four-bit numbers, four adders are connected in parallel as shown for the addition of 1110 (14) and 0111 (7) to give a sum of 10101 (21). By joining more full-adders to the left end of the system, numbers with more bits can be added. In the block diagram for a four-bit adder the binary weightings (i.e. 16, 8, 4, 2, 1) of the inputs and outputs are given.

(b) 4008B four-bit full adder

This IC adds two four-bit binary numbers which are applied to inputs $A_4A_3A_2A_1$ and $B_4B_3B_2B_1$, with A_1 and B_1 being for the least significant bits. The sum is given by outputs $C_0S_4S_3S_2S_1$ where C_0 is the 'carry out' and S_1 the least significant bit. For larger bit numbers, 'carry out' is connected to 'carry in' of another adder which deals with the next four most significant bits. Otherwise 'carry in' is kept 'low'.

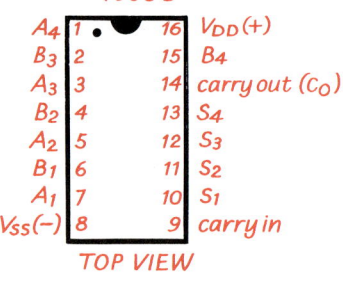

Project 8 (*Electronic adder*) uses this IC.

(c) 4585B four-bit magnitude comparator

Two four-bit binary numbers A and B are compared, each number having four parallel inputs $A_4A_3A_2A_1$ and $B_4B_3B_2B_1$, A_1 and B_1 being for the least significant bits.

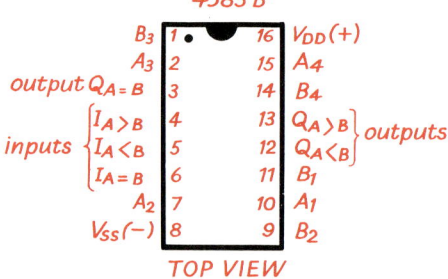

There are three outputs. If $A > B$, $Q_{A>B}$ goes 'high', if $A < B$, $Q_{A<B}$ goes 'high', if $A = B$, $Q_{A=B}$ goes 'high'. For example, if A is 1000 (8) and B is 0100 (4), then $Q_{A>B}$ gives a 'high' output but if B is also 1000 (8) then the $Q_{A=B}$ output is 'high'.

In normal operation inputs $I_{A>B}$ and $I_{A<B}$ are kept 'low', while $I_{A=B}$ is made 'high'. (These inputs are used to allow expansion when two or more comparators are connected.)

This IC is used in Project 7 (*Computer space invaders*).

Code converters

Digital electronic systems use the binary code; we find the decimal one more convenient. A code converter changes numbers in one code into another. An *encoder* makes conversions into binary, often from decimal. A *decoder* does the reverse.

(a) Code conversion Many methods of code conversion are used but the basic principles can be understood from the diagram below. It shows how the decimal numbers 1 to 9 can be encoded into binary using four multi-input OR gates. For example, when switch 3 is closed, one input to OR_1 is connected to V_{DD} and goes 'high', as does one input to OR_2. All other inputs stay 'low' since they go to ground via one of the resistors. Outputs Q_1 and Q_2 therefore go 'high' (page 7), while Q_3 and Q_4 remain 'low'. The binary output is then 0011 (=3). Check that the correct 'bit' patterns are obtained from $Q_4Q_3Q_2Q_1$ when each of the other switches is closed.

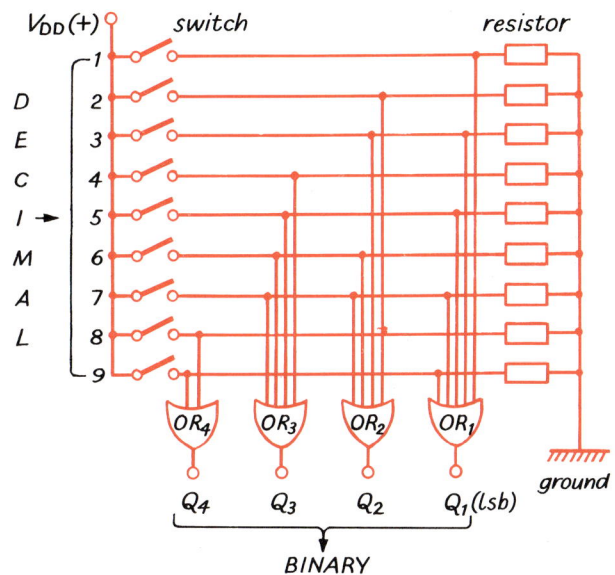

Decoders work on similar principles with the binary digit supplying the inputs to appropriate logic gates.

(b) 74C922 keyboard encoder This 18-pin IC encodes a hexadecimal (16) input into a four-bit binary output. The inputs are supplied from sixteen switches (marked 0 to 9 and A to F), connected in a matrix of four rows and four columns so that only eight connections have to be made to the IC – since it has eight inputs.

$C1$ is an external capacitor whose value (e.g. $0.01\,\mu F$) decides the rate of scanning of the switches, by a fast oscillator in the IC, to detect the one that has been pressed. The other external capacitor $C2$ (e.g. $0.1\,\mu F$) eliminates 'contact bounce' on the switches; this occurs when two contacts are pushed together. They do not stay in contact at first but make a series of rapid, imperfect contacts which produce random, unwanted pulses. The IC contains a circuit (except for $C2$) to prevent this.

Normally data available (DA) and output enable (OE) are kept 'low', as in Project 8 (*Electronic adder*).

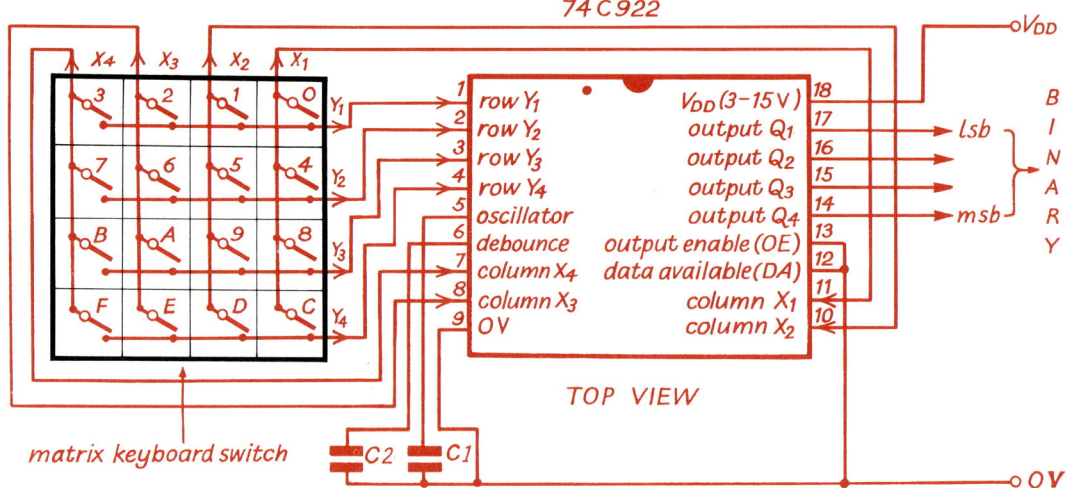

(c) 4511B BCD decoder-driver-latch BCD numbers applied to the four inputs $A_4 A_3 A_2$ and A_1 (lsb) are converted into their decimal equivalents. Seven decoded outputs a,b,c,d,e,f,g are produced, each capable of driving directly one segment of a 7-segment LED decimal display *with suitable current-limiting resistors* (page 23). For example, if $A_4 = 0$, $A_3 = 0$, $A_2 = 1$ and $A_1 = 1$, the BCD input is 0011 (=3) and the five outputs a,b,c,d,g needed to light the five LED segments making a '3' on the display, go 'high'. If the BCD number exceeds 9, all outputs go 'low' and the display is blank.

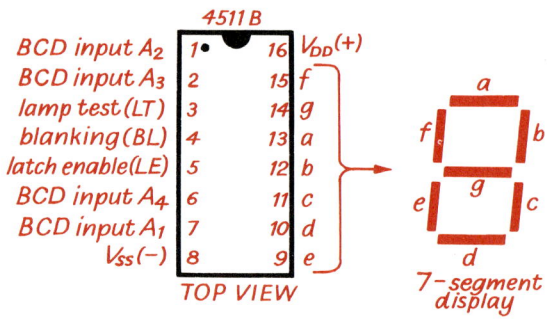

Normally LT is kept 'high'; if it is 'low' all seven outputs go 'high' (and test the display by lighting every segment) no matter what the conditions are on $A_4 A_3 A_2 A_1$. BL is also usually held 'high', but if it goes 'low' (and LT is 'high'), all outputs go 'low' and blank out the display.

When LE is 'low' the state of the seven outputs is decided by the data at the four inputs, i.e. they follow the input changes. If LE is 'high', the last data at $A_4 A_3 A_2 A_1$ is stored or 'latched' and held on the display.

The table sums up the behaviour of the IC.

LT	BL	LE	\multicolumn{4}{c|}{BCD inputs}	\multicolumn{7}{c|}{Outputs}	Display
			A_4	A_3	A_2	A_1	a	b	c	d	e	f	g	
0	X	X	X	X	X	X	1	1	1	1	1	1	1	8
1	0	X	X	X	X	X	0	0	0	0	0	0	0	blank
1	1	0	0	0	1	1	1	1	1	1	0	0	1	3
1	1	0	1	0	1	0	0	0	0	0	0	0	0	blank
1	1	1	X	X	X	X	\multicolumn{7}{c|}{*}	*

X = does not matter if 1 or 0
★ = stores BCD input present when LE last 0

Displays

A display shows the state or 'logic level' of the output of a digital device, i.e. whether it is 'high' (a '1') or 'low' (a '0').

(a) Light-emitting diode (LED) When forward biased, an LED conducts and emits red, yellow or green light depending on the composition of the gallium arsenide phosphide from which it is made. Unless it is the 'constant-current' type, *it requires an external series resistor* to limit the current (typically 2–20 mA). On a 9 V supply, 680 Ω is suitable. The voltage drop across a conducting LED is 1.7 V. Reverse voltages of more than 5 V may cause damage. The lead nearest the 'flat' is the cathode.

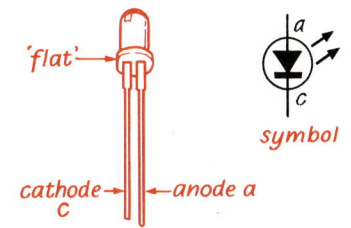

In a simple display, one LED represents one bit, several being used for a multi-bit binary output, as in Project 7. One arrangement is shown for detecting a '1' output and another for a '0' output from, for example, a logic gate. In the first, the gate acts as a 'source' of the LED current and in the second, it has to be able to accept or 'sink' the current. In general, the output from a CMOS IC will drive an LED directly but it is better practice, especially if other ICs are being driven from the same output, to use a transistor (e.g. ZTX300) as shown, to avoid 'overloading' which might stop switching.

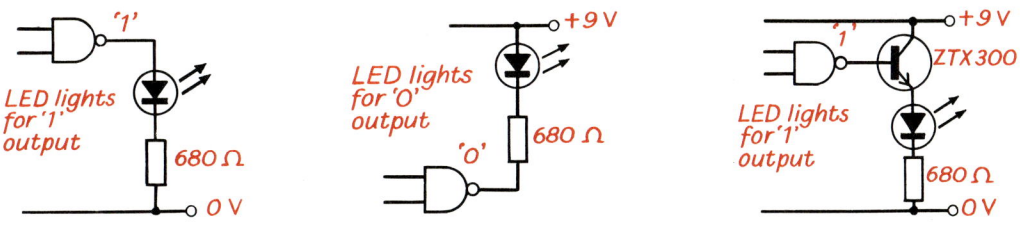

(b) Decimal display A popular type consists of seven small, bar-shaped LED segments arranged as a figure 8 so that, depending on which combinations are energized, the numbers 0 to 9 light up. All the LED cathodes (or sometimes anodes) are joined to form a common connection. Current limiting resistors are required (e.g. 270 Ω), preferably one per segment.

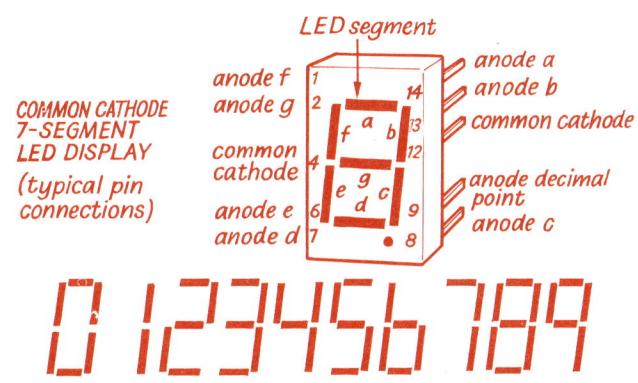

23

Building circuits

(a) Circuit boards The board shown accepts ICs as well as discrete components.

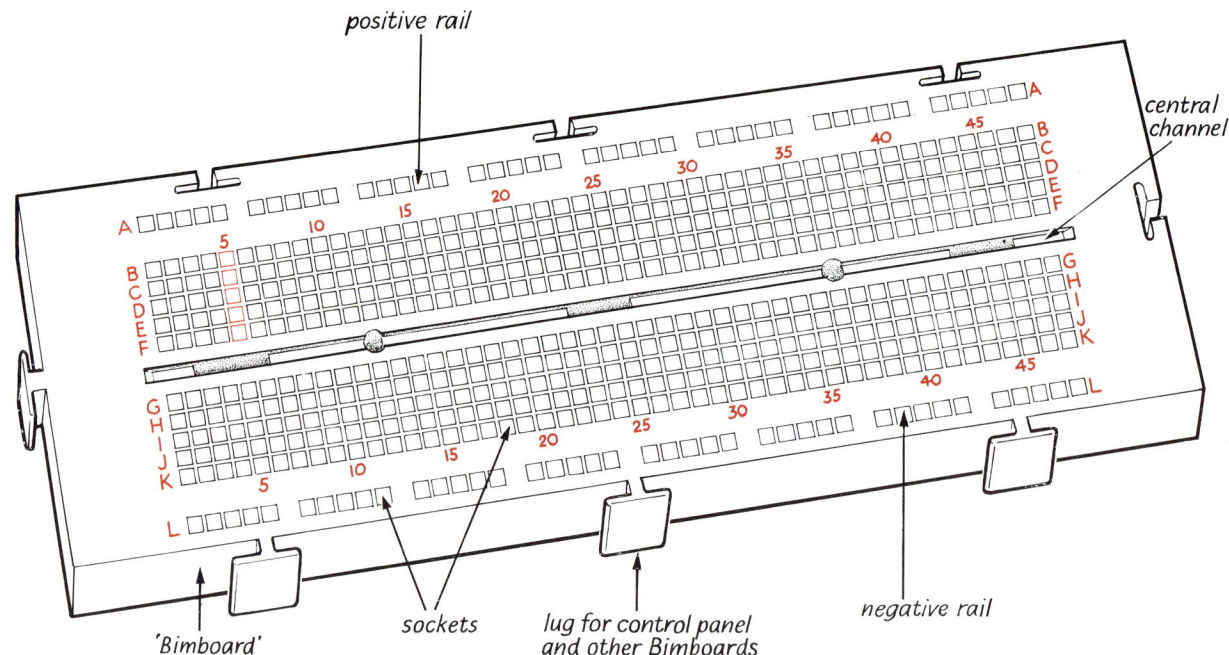

It has 47 rows of 5 interconnected sockets, 0.1 inch apart, on each side of a central channel across which d.i.l. ICs can be fitted. A wire inserted in a socket in a certain row becomes connected to wires in any of the other 4 sockets in that row by a spring clip under the board. For example, wires in sockets B5, C5, D5, E5, and F5 (shown in colour) are all joined.

A row of 40 interconnected sockets along the top of the board and a similar row along the bottom act as the positive and negative power supply rails (called 'bus bars').

For all projects, two boards are linked together, either end to end or side by side. The linking is done in different ways with different boards. In the 'Bimboard', lugs on one fit into slots on the other. This type also has a useful vertically mounting removable control panel; where this is not provided one can be improvised.

(b) Battery A 9V PP3 type is suitable; one for a calculator, though more expensive, will last longer. A battery clip connector makes connection to the board easy.

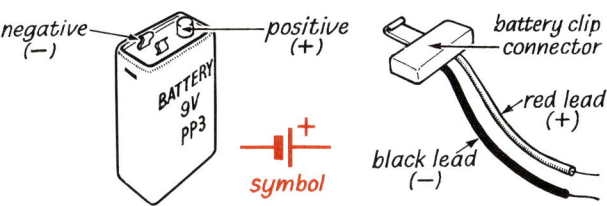

(c) Switches Three types used in the projects are shown. All have pin spacings which suit the 0.1 inch separation of circuit board sockets.

SLIDE SWITCH SPDT (single pole double throw)

KEYBOARD PUSH SWITCH

DUAL-IN-LINE 4-SPST SWITCHES (single pole single throw)

(d) Resistors The examples below show how the coloured bands on a resistor (-⊏⊐-) give its resistance in ohms (Ω) and its tolerance.

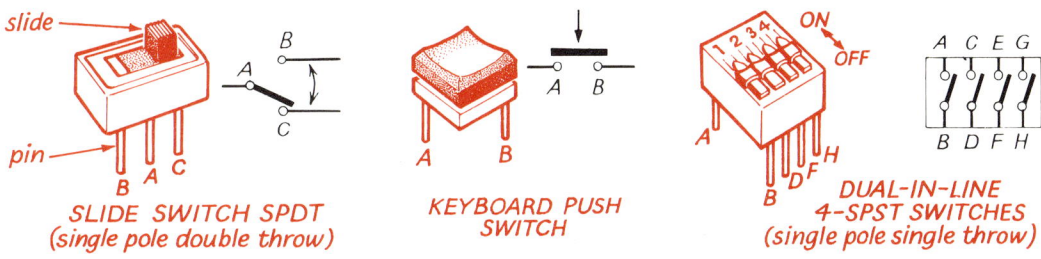

Number	Colour
0	black
1	brown
2	red
3	orange
4	yellow
5	green
6	blue
7	violet
8	grey
9	white

{ rainbow (colours 2–7) }

1st number — 2nd number — number of 0's — tolerance
gold ± 5%
silver ± 10%
no band ± 20%

brown (1), black (0), brown (0) = 100 Ω
yellow (4), violet (7), red (00) = 4700 Ω = 4.7 kΩ
red (2), red (2), green (00000) = 2 200 000 = 2.2 MΩ

25

(e) Capacitors Capacitance values are measured in microfarads (μF), nanofarads (nF) and picofarads (pF): $1\,\mu$F = 1000 nF and 1 nF =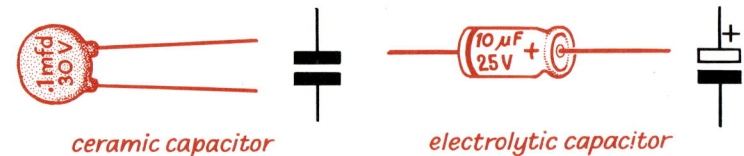

ceramic capacitor   electrolytic capacitor

1000 pF. Two common values of ceramic capacitors are $0.1\,\mu$F (often marked wrongly as .1 mfd) and $0.01\,\mu$F (10 nF). They are made with a variety of shapes and markings. Electrolytic capacitors must be connected so that the conventional current flows into their + terminal. The greatest voltage a capacitor can withstand is marked on it, e.g. 30 V.

(f) Transistors The ZTX 300 is an npn transistor. It must be connected correctly with the collector to the positive (+) of the battery and the emitter to the negative (−).

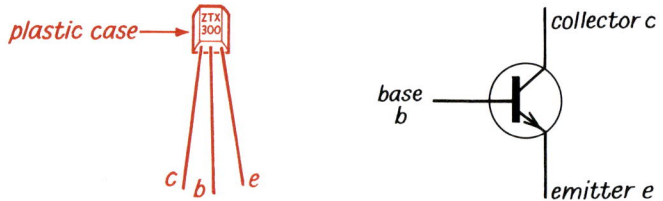

(g) Connecting wire PVC-covered tinned copper wire with one solid wire of diameter 0.6 mm ($1/0.6$ mm) is suitable. The PVC insulation can be removed from the ends either with wire strippers or using a pair of blunt-nosed pliers and a pair of side cutters as shown. With practice you should be able to judge just how much the side cutters have to be *squeezed* and *pulled* to remove the insulation without cutting the wire.

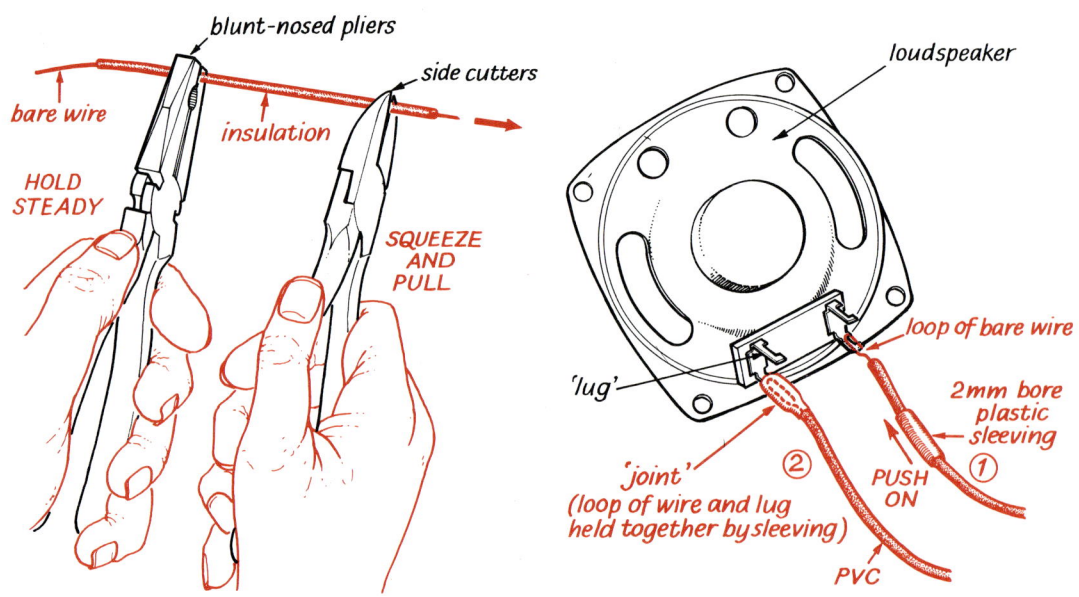

(h) Making 'joints' Wires can be connected to the 'lugs' on a loudspeaker using a small piece of 2 mm bore plastic sleeving – as shown by ① and ② above. Joints with LEDs mounted on a control panel can be made in the same way with 1 mm sleeving.

(i) Wiring the circuit board To connect a wire to the board push about 1 cm of the *bare* end *straight* into the socket (not at an angle) so that it is gripped by the spring clip under the board. Do not use wires that are *dirty* or have *kinked* ends. Only put one wire in each socket.

Resistors and capacitors can be mounted either horizontally or vertically by *carefully* bending the leads as shown.

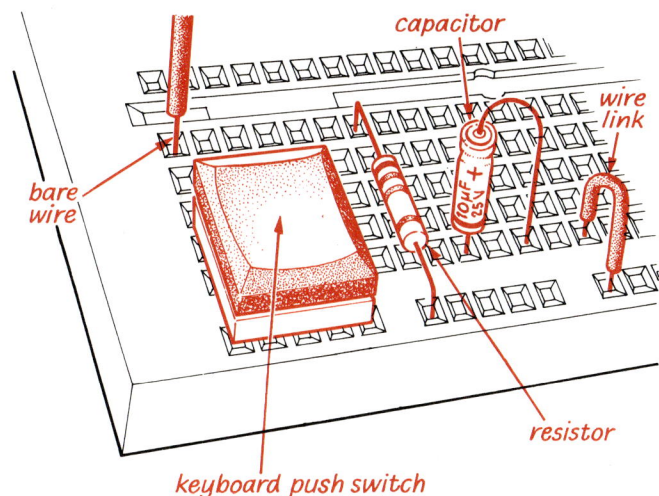

KEEP WIRES SHORT AND LAID OUT NEATLY TO MAKE CHECKING EASY.

1 Electronic shooting gallery

The target is a 'light' moving rapidly along a row of seven LEDs (six red and a green one in the centre) fed by seven (of the ten) outputs from a decade counter driven by an astable. When a 'shot is fired', by pressing and releasing a push switch, the motion stops leaving one LED alight. If it is the green one, you have made a 'hit' which is indicated by another light (a yellow LED) coming on and also by a brief burst of sound from a loudspeaker. After a few seconds the moving light starts again, ready for the next shot.

WHAT YOU NEED

Dual astable IC (556); astable IC (4047B); decade counter IC (4017B); quad 2-input NAND gate (4011B); four npn transistors (ZTX300); eight LEDs (six red, one green, one yellow); keyboard push switch; resistors – 100 Ω (brown black brown), two 680 Ω (blue grey brown), two 10 kΩ (brown black orange), two 100 kΩ (brown black yellow), 220 kΩ (red red yellow), 470 kΩ (yellow violet yellow), 2.2 MΩ (red red green); ceramic capacitors – three 0.01 μF, two 0.1 μF; electrolytic capacitors – 1 μF, 4.7 μF; loudspeaker 2½ in, 25 to 80 Ω; 9 V battery; battery clip connector; two circuit boards; PVC-covered tinned copper wire 1/0.6 mm.

HERE IS THE CIRCUIT

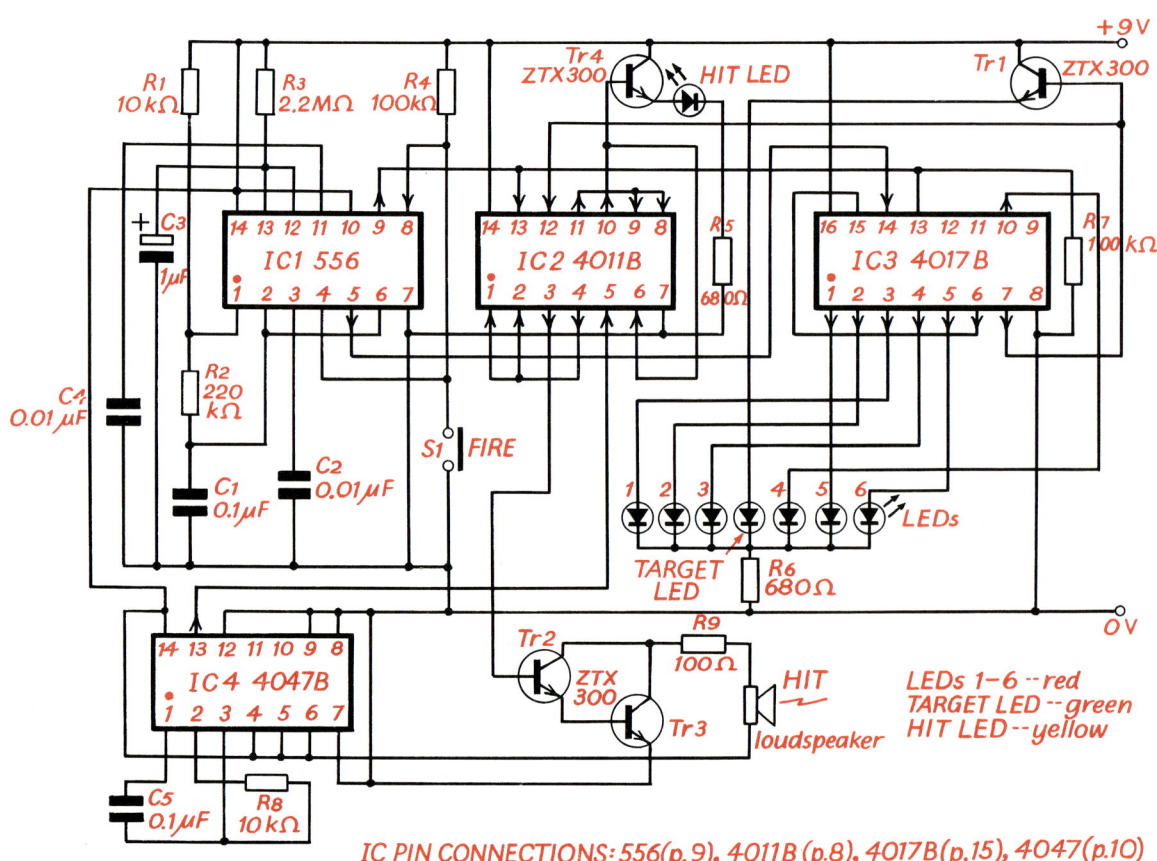

IC PIN CONNECTIONS: 556 (p.9), 4011B (p.8), 4017B (p.15), 4047 (p.10)

HOW TO BUILD IT

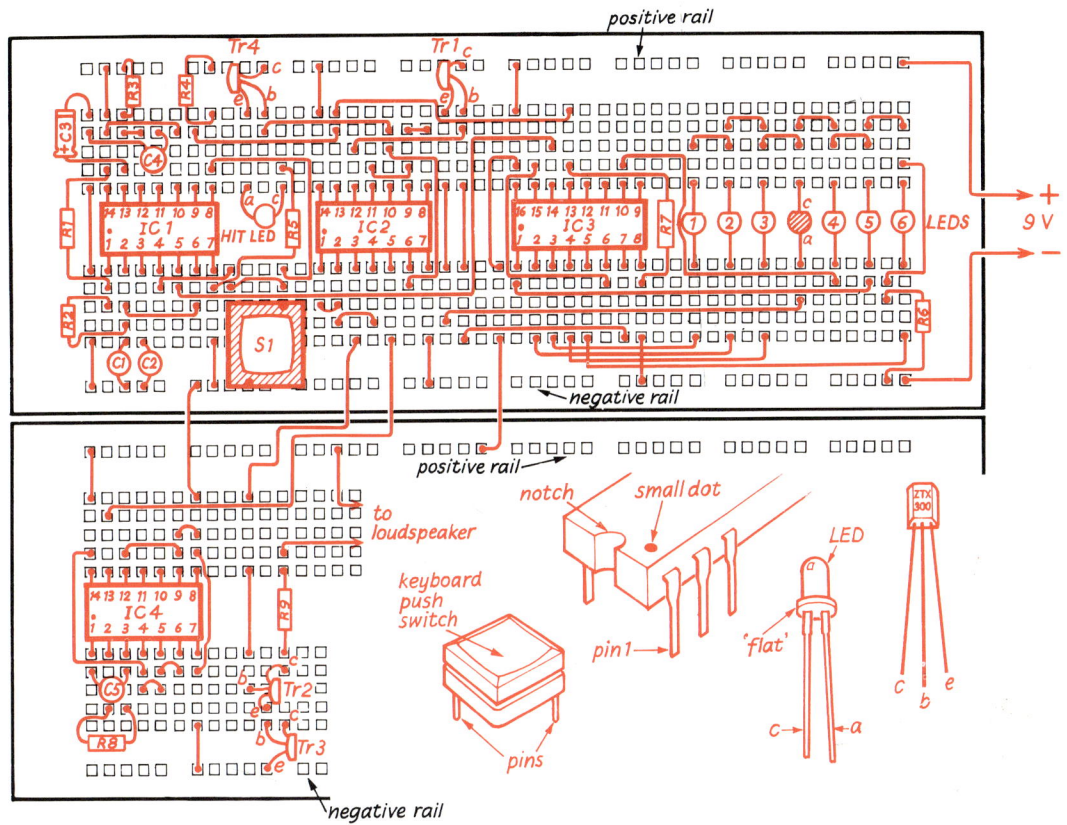

1. Couple two circuit boards together, side by side.
2. Identify pin 1 on the ICs from the small dot or notch at one end of the case. Carefully push each IC into the circuit board in the positions shown, taking care not to bend the pins in the process.
3. Insert wire links from each IC to the positive and negative rails and between other sockets, as shown.
4. Insert R1 to R7, C1 to C4, and S1 into the board. Be sure that C3 is connected the correct way round; the + end has a groove and the − end a black band (usually).
5. Insert the eight LEDs as shown, remembering that the cathode is next to the 'flat' at the bottom of the plastic case.
6. Identify the collector (c), base (b) and emitter (e) leads on transistors Tr1 and Tr4. Insert them in the circuit board, making sure they are exactly as shown.
7. CHECK THE CIRCUIT CAREFULLY.
8. Connect the battery with the *correct polarity*. The 'light' should move along the row of LEDs from 1 to 6; if any don't light, they may be the wrong way round. You can now 'fire' a test shot by pressing S1. When you get a 'hit', the yellow LED should light up for a few seconds before the target starts moving again.
9. Disconnect the battery. Complete the circuit by adding R8, R9, C5, Tr2, Tr3 and the loudspeaker. Reconnect the battery. A 'hit' should now also be 'announced' by the loudspeaker.

HOW IT WORKS

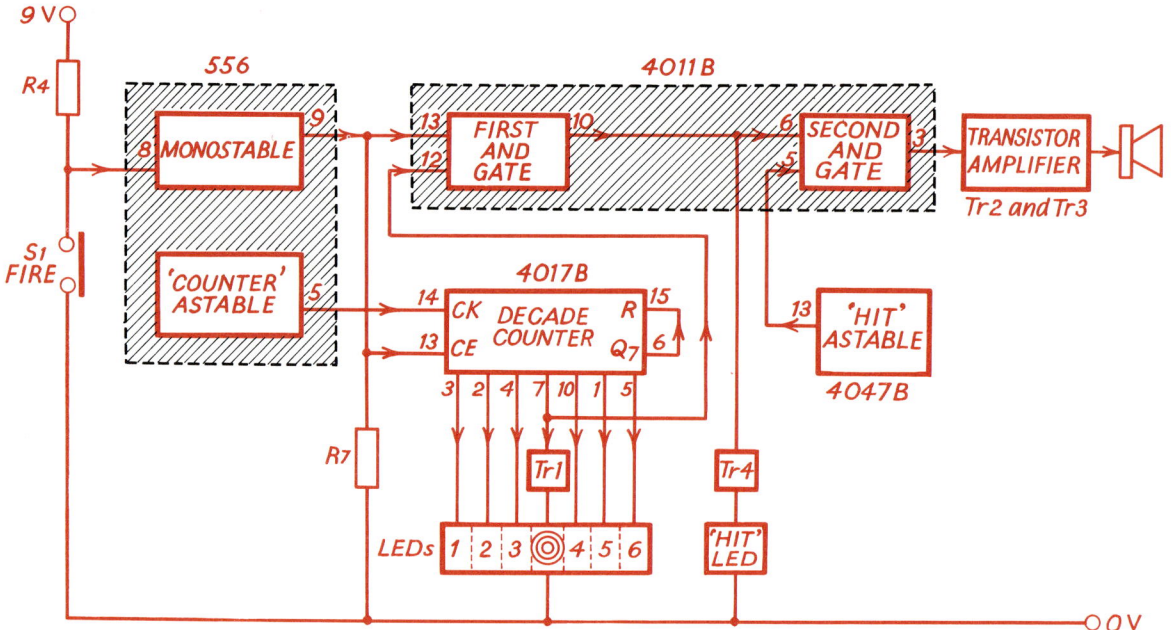

When the battery is connected, the output (pin 5) of the COUNTER ASTABLE sends pulses at a rate determined by $R1$, $R2$ and $C1$ (about 30 Hz, see page 10) to the 'clock' input (pin 14) of the DECADE COUNTER. The latter counts the pulses, i.e. its outputs go 'high' in turn since 'clock enable' (pin 13) is 'low' (being connected to 0 V by $R7$). The light therefore seems to move along the row of seven LEDs. The eighth pulse makes the eighth output (Q_7, pin 6), which is connected to 'reset' (pin 15), go 'high'. As a result the DECADE COUNTER resets to zero and starts counting up to 7 again and so on.

When the FIRE switch $S1$ is pressed (momentarily), the 'trigger' input (pin 8) on the MONOSTABLE falls from 9 V (to which it is normally connected via $R4$) to 0 V. The resulting *falling edge* (⊓) triggers the MONOSTABLE and makes it produce an output pulse (⊓ ; pin 9) lasting for a time determined by $R3$ and $C3$ (about 3 seconds, see page 10). This pulse has two effects.

First, it makes 'clock enable' (pin 13) on the DECADE COUNTER go 'high' and so stops the counting (page 15) leaving one LED alight. Second, it causes one input (pin 13) of the FIRST AND GATE to go 'high'. The other input (pin 12) on this gate will also be 'high' if output Q_3 (pin 7) on the DECADE COUNTER is 'high', i.e. if the TARGET LED is the LED left alight when the counting stopped (showing a 'hit' has been made). In that case, with both inputs 'high', the output (pin 10) from the FIRST AND GATE will be 'high' (page 7) and the HIT LED lights up – for as long as the MONOSTABLE pulse keeps the first input (pin 13) 'high'.

The announcement of a 'hit' by the loudspeaker occurs as follows. One input (pin 6) to the SECOND AND GATE goes 'high' when the output (pin 10) of the FIRST AND GATE goes 'high'. The other input (pin 5) is supplied by the output (pin 13) from the HIT ASTABLE which produces pulses at a rate determined by $R8$ and $C5$ (about 230 Hz, see page 10) as soon as the battery is connected. The output (pin 3) of the SECOND AND GATE becomes 'high' when both its inputs are 'high', that is, while the MONOSTABLE pulse lasts. This output is amplified by $Tr1$ and $Tr2$ (called a *Darlington pair*) before it produces a note of constant pitch (about 230 Hz) in the loudspeaker.

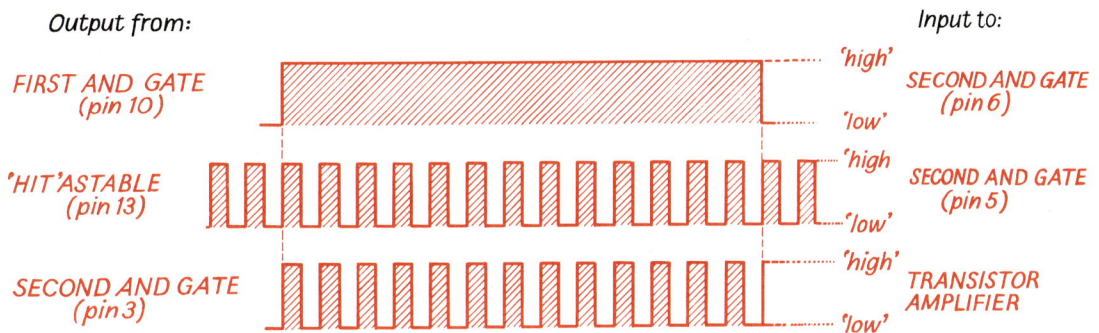

Notes. 1. Each AND GATE is made by combining two NAND gates (page 8).

2. *Tr*1 drives the TARGET LED and prevents overloading of output Q_3 (pin 7) of the DECADE COUNTER which has also to supply one input (pin 12) of the FIRST AND GATE.

THINGS TO TRY

1 What happens if you change $R2$ from 220 kΩ to 470 kΩ? Make the change and see if you are correct.

2 Work out what the effect will be of increasing $C3$ from 1 μF to 4.7 μF. Check your prediction.

3 How will the pitch of the 'hit note' from the loudspeaker be altered if you decrease $C5$ from 0.1 μF to 0.01 μF? Check your answer.

4 *Electronic darts.* If you give each of the seven LEDs a number, you can draw up rules for a game of electronic darts which are similar to those for ordinary darts. Do this and use the Shooting Gallery for that purpose.

2 Quiz-game switches

This circuit decides which of four contestants in a quiz game was first to press his or her answer switch. The contestant's light comes on, accompanied by a two-tone note from a loudspeaker, and prevents the other contestants from lighting theirs. When the question master presses the 'reset' switch, the light that was on, goes off and all is ready for the next question.

WHAT YOU NEED

Quad D latch IC (4042B); dual 4-input NOR gate IC (4002B); dual astable IC (556); four LEDs; five keyboard push switches (four blue, one red); resistors – 680 Ω (blue grey brown), 1 kΩ (brown black red), two 10 kΩ (brown black orange), 27 kΩ (red violet orange), six 100 kΩ (brown black yellow); ceramic capacitors – two 0.01 μF; electrolytic capacitors – 1 μF, 4.7 μF; loudspeaker 2½ in, 25 to 80 Ω; 9 V battery; battery clip connector; two circuit boards; PVC-covered tinned copper wire 1/0.6 mm.

HERE IS THE CIRCUIT

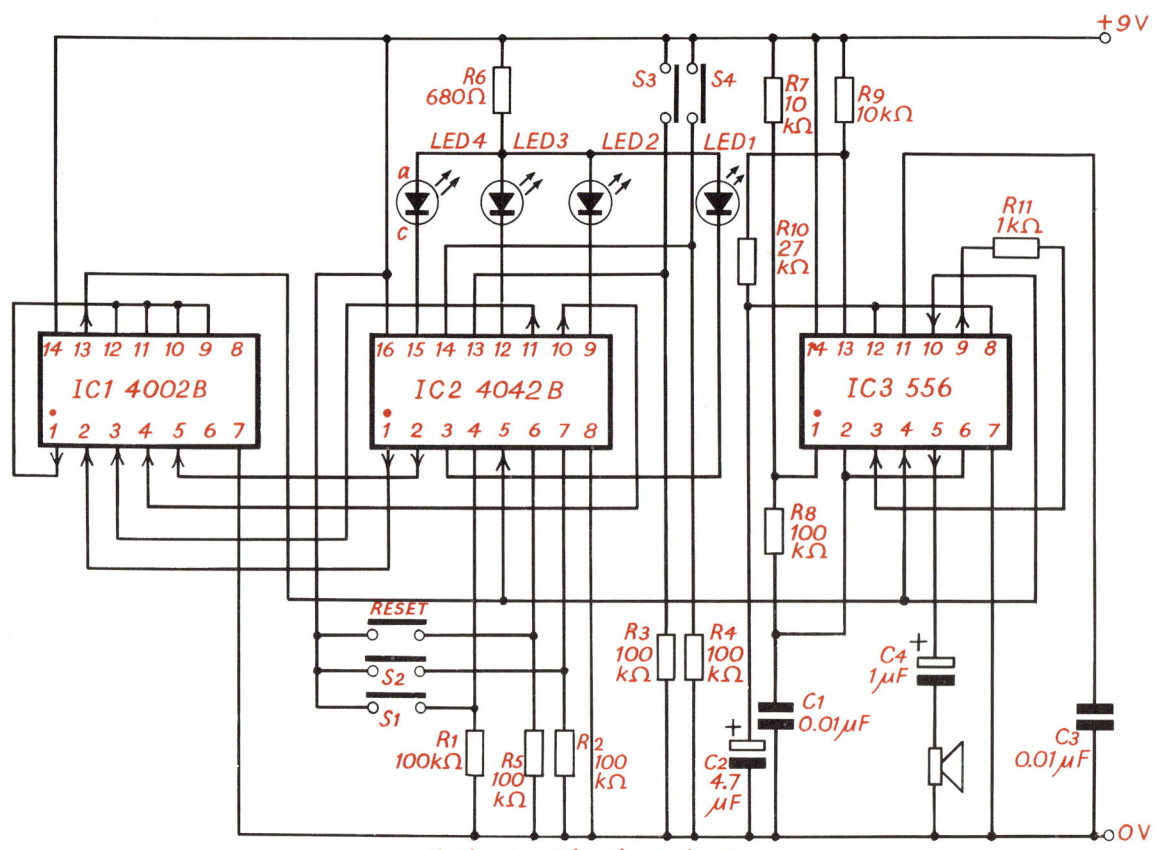

IC PIN CONNECTIONS: 4002B (p.8), 4042B (p.13), 556 (p.9)

HOW TO BUILD IT

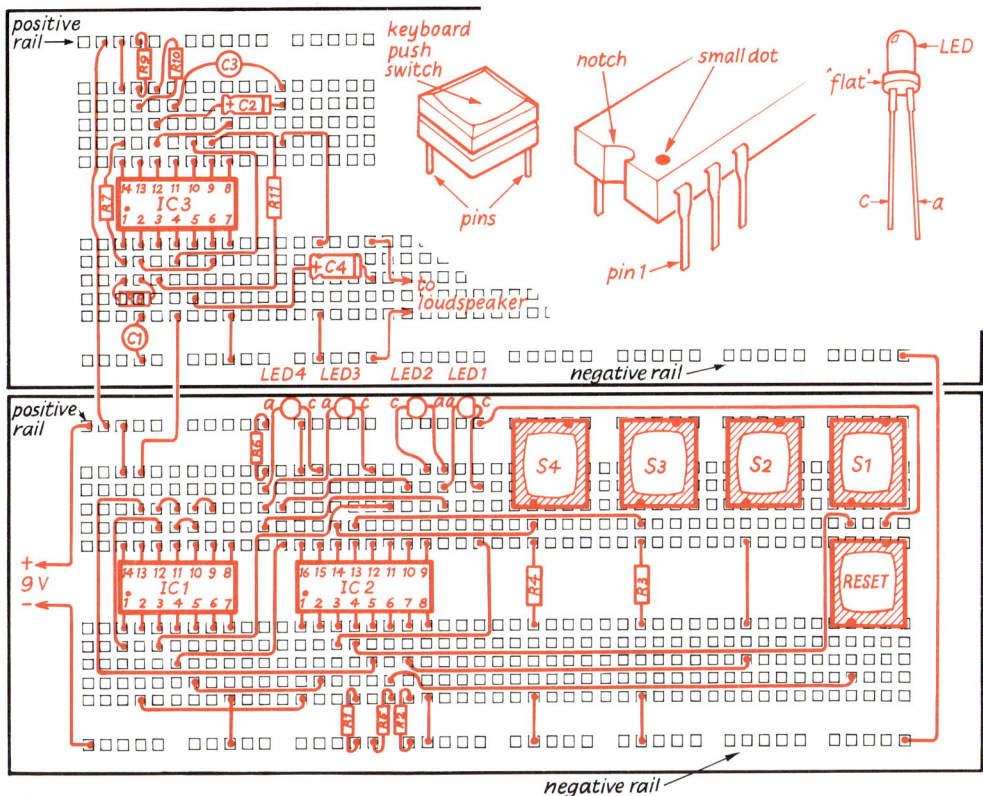

1. Couple two circuit boards together, side by side.
2. Identify pin 1 on the ICs from the small dot or notch at one end of the case. Carefully push each IC into the circuit board in the positions shown, taking care not to bend the pins in the process.
3. Insert wire links from each IC to the positive and negative rails and between other sockets, as shown.
4. Insert $R1$ to $R6$, $S1$ to $S4$ and the reset switch (taking care not to damage the pins).
5. Insert the four LEDs as shown, remembering that the cathode is next to the 'flat' at the bottom of the plastic case.
6. CHECK THE CIRCUIT CAREFULLY.
7. Connect the battery with the *correct polarity*. Press and release $S1$; LED 1 should light up. Check that none of the other LEDs light when $S2$, $S3$ and $S4$ are pressed in turn. Press the 'reset' switch; LED 1 should go out. Repeat this procedure three times more with the other contestants' switches, to ensure the other LEDs are connected the right way round and light up when the appropriate switch is pressed.
8. Disconnect the battery. Complete the circuit by adding $R7$ to $R11$, $C1$ to $C4$ and the loudspeaker. Be sure that $C2$ and $C4$ are connected the correct way round; the + end has a groove and the − end a black band (usually). Reconnect the battery. The loudspeaker should now 'warble' when any contestant's switch is pressed.

HOW IT WORKS

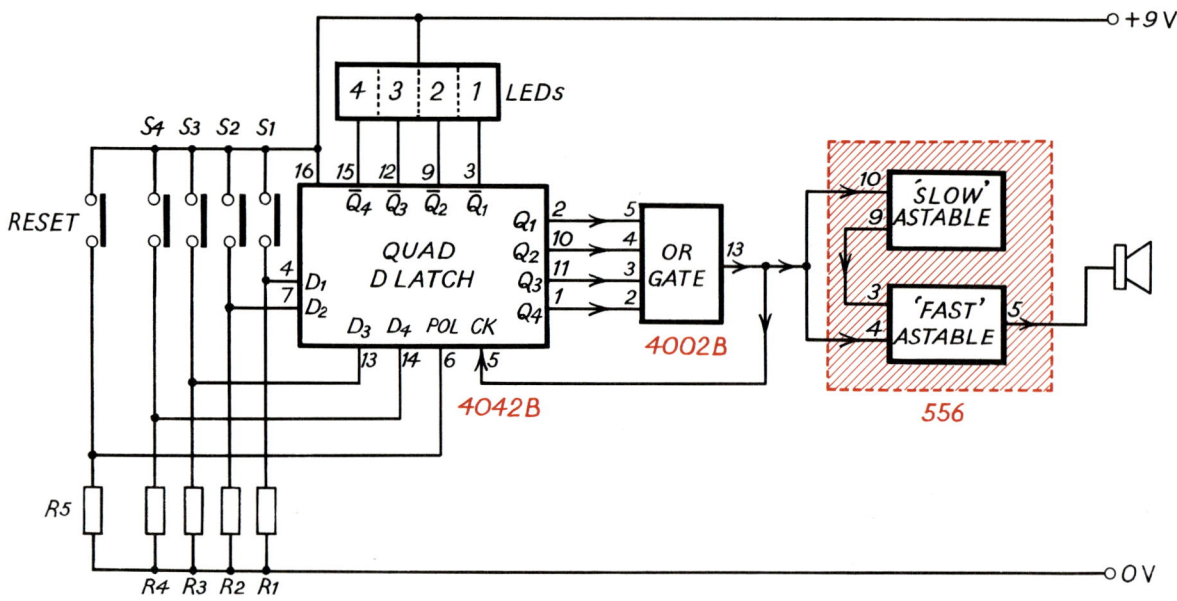

When S1, S2, S3 and S4 are open, the four data inputs D_1, D_2, D_3 and D_4 on the QUAD D LATCH are all 'low' because they are connected to 0V via R1, R2, R3 and R4 respectively. The 'polarity' input POL (pin 6) is also 'low' when the 'reset' switch is open, R5 providing the connection to 0 V in this case. The 'clock' input CK (pin 5) is normally 'low' and since POL and CK are *not different*, all four true outputs Q_1, Q_2, Q_3 and Q_4 have the same states as their corresponding D inputs, i.e. they are 'low' (page 13). The four complementary outputs $\bar{Q}_1$, $\bar{Q}_2$, $\bar{Q}_3$ and $\bar{Q}_4$ are therefore all 'high', which means both ends of each LED are 'high', i.e. the LEDs do not light up since they are not forward biased.

If S1 is pressed, D_1 goes 'high' (now being connected to 9 V), causing Q_1 to go 'high'. Also, it makes $\bar{Q}_1$ go 'low', thus lighting LED 1 by 'sinking' the current from the 9 V supply, i.e. LED 1 detects a '0' at $\bar{Q}_1$ (page 23). At the same time, the output from the OR gate (pin 13) goes 'high' because one of its inputs (from Q_1 on the LATCH) has gone 'high' (page 7). CK and POL are now *different*. This 'latches' all the LEDs,

that is, they retain the states they are in and no change can occur even if the states of any of the D inputs are changed by other contestants' switches being pressed. All this happens in a fraction of a second.

The LEDs are reset (none lit) by pressing the 'reset' switch so making POL 'high', i.e. the same as CK. The Q outputs then take the same states as their D inputs again – namely 'low' if all the contestant switches are open.

The two-tone effect from the loudspeaker is produced by using both halves of the 556 ASTABLE. The 'lower' half acts as a 'fast' astable generating square pulses at a rate fixed by R7, R8 and C1 (about 700 Hz, page 10). The 'upper' half operates as a 'slow' astable, its pulse rate being decided by R9, R10 and C2 (about 8 Hz). These 'slow', square pulses (at pin 9) are applied to the 'control voltage' (pin 3) of the 'fast' astable via R11 and *frequency modulate* its output (page 10), i.e. the frequency of its output pulses changes abruptly from 700 Hz or so to a higher value and back to 700 Hz again about eight times a second. All the above occurs when the output from the

OR gate goes 'high' since it makes 'reset' on both astables (pins 4 and 10) go 'high', i.e. above the 0.7 V needed to make them work (page 10).

Note. The OR gate is made by connecting one of the two NOR gates in the 4002B as a NOT gate (i.e. joining all its four inputs together) and applying the output from the other NOR gate to the one input so formed.

THINGS TO TRY

1 *Using low voltage filament lamps instead of LEDs.* These give more light than LEDs. This

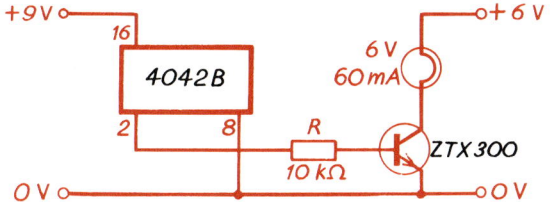

is something you can investigate if you have a 6 V 60 mA lamp and holder and a 6 V battery (or a 4.5 V will do). The circuit shows a lamp driven by the Q_1 output (pin 2) on the 4042B via a ZTX300 transistor. The circuits for driving lamps from the other three Q outputs would be the same. Note that the negative terminal of the lamp battery has to be joined to the negative rail of the circuit boards. R protects the transistor from excessive base currents.

2 *Waiting-room sign.* In, for example, a doctor's waiting room three signs can be lit to read 'Enter', 'Wait' and 'Engaged' so that it is impossible to have more than one on at a time.

The lights are controlled by four switches (one for 'reset') in the doctor's surgery. Modify the Quiz-game circuit so that it operates as a Waiting-room sign using a green, a yellow and a red LED for the three signs.

3 Two-way traffic lights I

Traffic at cross-roads needs two-way control. This model of British traffic signals provides that and also keeps the red and green lights on for longer than the yellow, as in the real case. The timing sequence is produced by an astable driving two flip-flops.

WHAT YOU NEED

Astable IC (4047B); dual D flip-flop IC (4013B); quad 2-input NAND gate IC (4011B); quad 2-input NOR gate IC (4001B); three npn transistors (ZTX300); six LEDs (two red, two yellow, two green); resistors – six 680 Ω (blue grey brown), 2.2 MΩ (red red green); ceramic capacitor – 0.1 µF; 9 V battery; battery clip connector; two circuit boards; PVC-covered tinned copper wire 1/0.6 mm.

HERE IS THE CIRCUIT

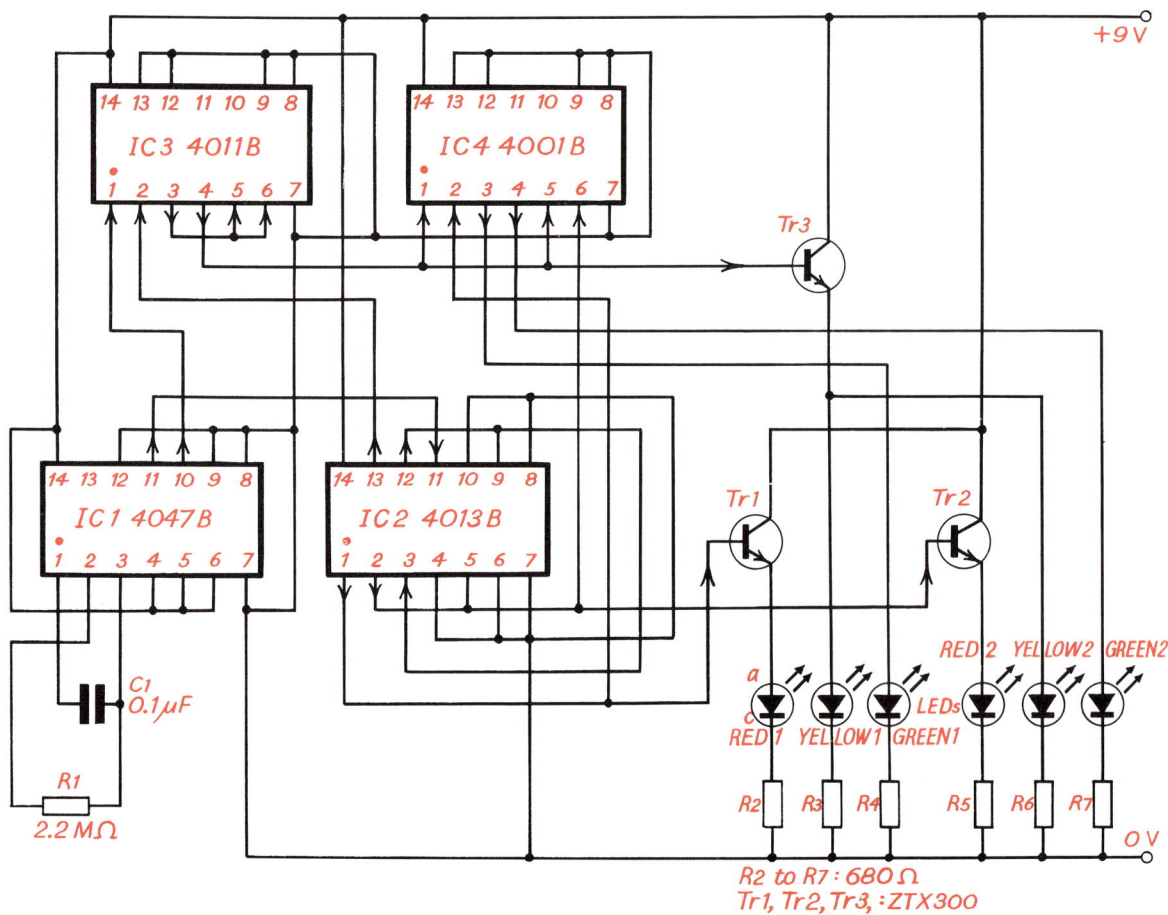

IC PIN CONNECTIONS: 4047B(p.10), 4013B(p.12), 4011B(p.8), 4001B(p.8)

HOW TO BUILD IT

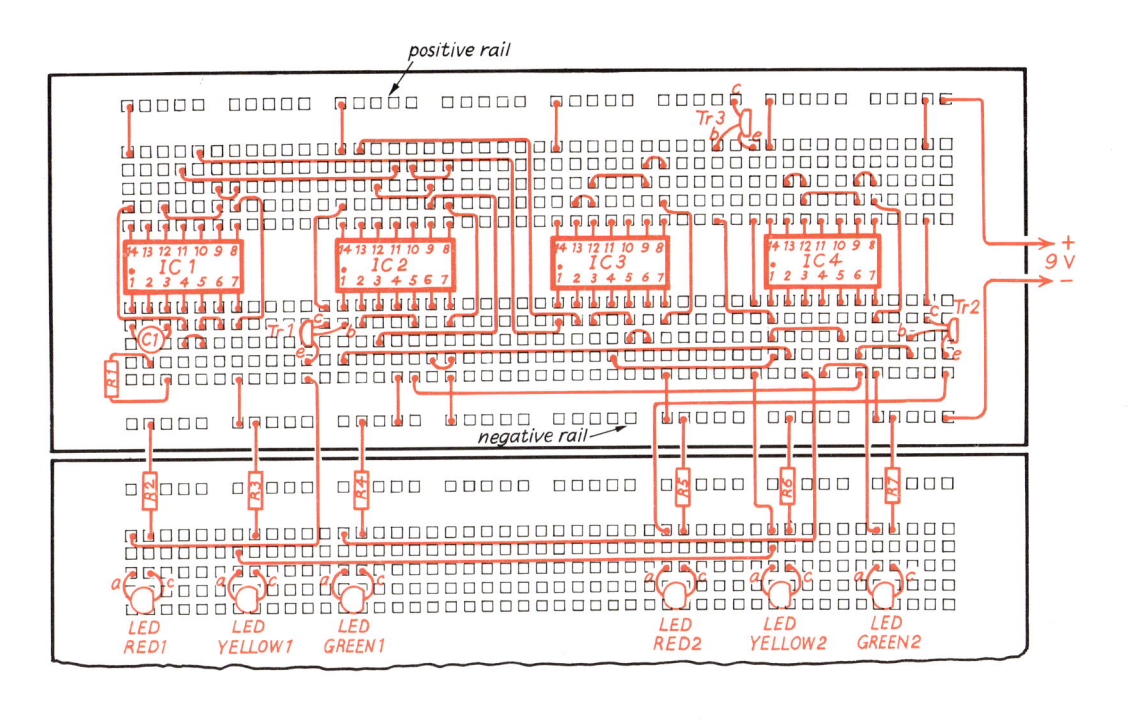

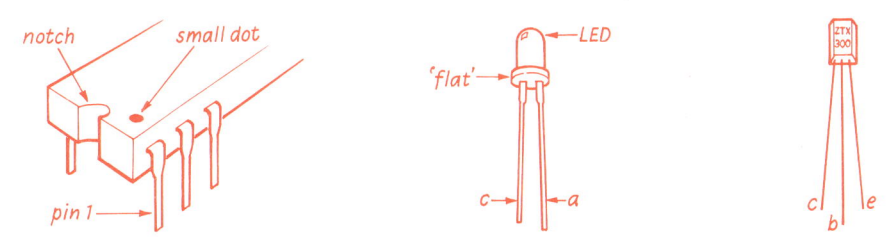

1 Couple two circuit boards together, side by side.
2 Identify pin 1 on the ICs from the small dot or notch at one end of the case. Carefully push each IC into the circuit board in the positions shown, taking care not to bend the pins in the process.
3 Insert wire links from each IC to the positive and negative rails and between other sockets, as shown.
4 Insert $R1$ to $R7$ and $C1$.
5 Identify the collector (c), base (b) and emitter (e) leads on the three transistors. Insert them in the circuit board, exactly as shown, making sure that the leads are not touching one another.
6 Insert the six LEDs as shown, remembering that the cathode is next to the 'flat' at the bottom of the plastic case.
7 CHECK THE CIRCUIT CAREFULLY.
8 Connect the battery with the *correct polarity*. The LEDs should light in the order shown in the truth table (page 39) where 1 represents a lit LED and 0 an unlit one. If any LEDs don't light when they should, they may be wrongly connected.

HOW IT WORKS

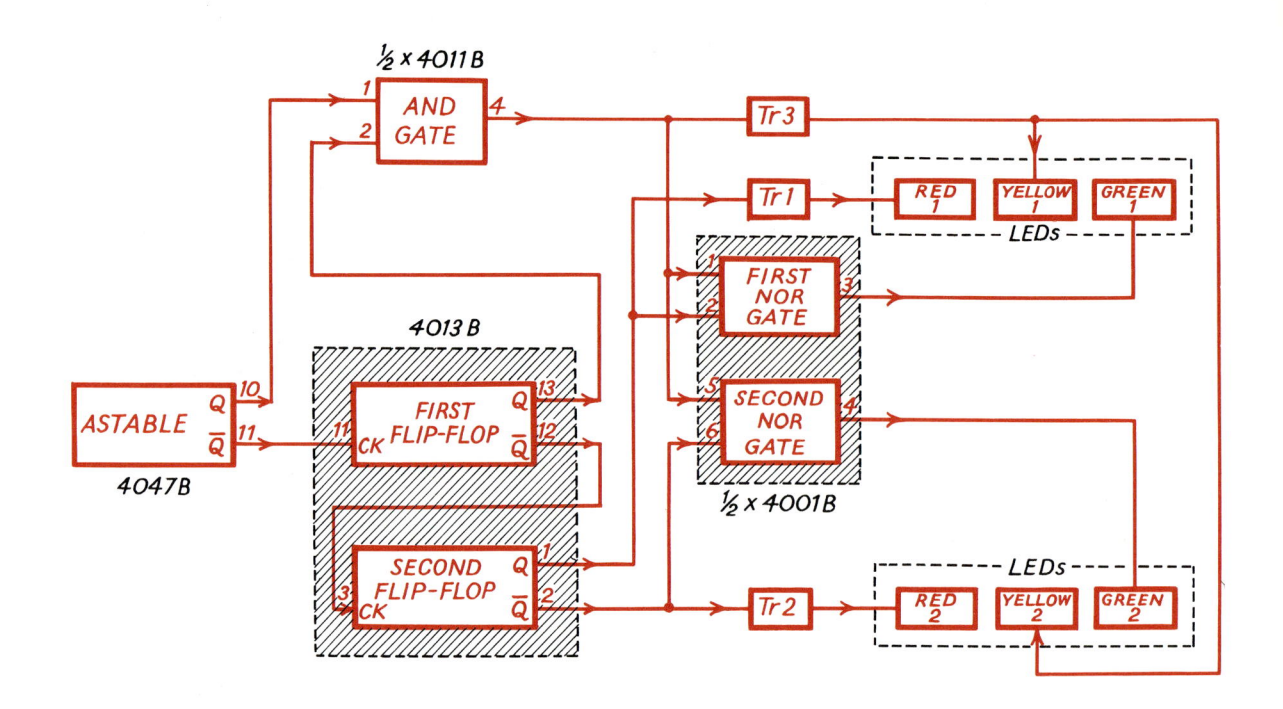

The block diagram is shown above. In the timing diagram opposite, line 1 shows the slow, square pulses from the Q output (pin 10) of the ASTABLE. The rate at which they are produced depends on $R1$ and $C1$ (page 10). These pulses provide one input to the AND GATE (pin 1).

Line 2 shows the $\bar{Q}$ output (pin 11) from the ASTABLE which supplies the 'clock' input CK (pin 11) of the FIRST FLIP-FLOP. The Q output of the latter (pin 13) is shown on line 3; it has *half* the frequency of the astable pulses and is applied to the second input (pin 2) of the AND GATE. Note that a change of state from 'low' to 'high' or vice versa occurs on the *rising* edge (⎍) of the $\bar{Q}$ pulses from the ASTABLE which are triggering it (page 12).

The output from the AND GATE (pin 4) is given in line 4. You can see that it is only 'high', i.e. LEDs Yellow 1 and 2 alight, when the pulses in lines 1 and 3 are *both* 'high' (page 7). $Tr3$ (as well as $Tr1$ and $Tr2$) prevent overloading problems (page 23).

Line 5 shows the $\bar{Q}$ output (pin 12) of the FIRST FLIP-FLOP. It supplies the 'clock' input CK (pin 3) to the SECOND FLIP-FLOP and triggers it (as before) on a rising edge to produce a Q output at pin 1 of the latter, which as line 6 shows, has *half* the frequency of the 'clock' pulses. When 'high' it lights LED Red 1.

The Q output from the SECOND FLIP-FLOP and the output from the AND GATE provide the two inputs to the FIRST NOR GATE. When these are both 'low', the output (pin 3) from the FIRST NOR GATE is 'high' and lights LED Green 1. Line 7 represents this output; it is obtained from lines 4 and 6.

The $\bar{Q}$ output (pin 2) from the SECOND FLIP-FLOP is shown in line 8. It controls LED Red 2 and along with the output from the AND GATE, it provides the input to the SECOND NOR GATE. The output from the latter is 'high' and lights LED Green 2, when both inputs are 'low'; it is obtained by comparing lines 4 and 8 and is given in line 9.

Notes. 1. Both flip-flops are used in the 'toggling mode' (page 12) with data inputs D connected to the corresponding $\bar{Q}$ outputs, i.e. pin 2 to pin 5 and pin 9 to pin 12.

2. The AND gate is made by combining two NAND gates with one having both inputs connected to form a NOT gate (page 8).

TIMING DIAGRAM

Line	Output from:		input to:
1	ASTABLE Q (pin 10)		AND GATE (pin 1)
2	ASTABLE Q̄ (pin 11)		1st FLIP-FLOP (pin 11)
3	1st FLIP-FLOP Q (pin 13)		AND GATE (pin 2)
4	AND GATE (pin 4)		BOTH NOR GATES: Tr3 (pins 1 and 5)
5	1st FLIP-FLOP Q̄ (pin 12)		2nd FLIP-FLOP (pin 3)
6	2nd FLIP-FLOP Q (pin 1)		1st NOR GATE: Tr1 (pin 2)
7	1st NOR GATE (pin 3)		LED GREEN 1
8	2nd FLIP-FLOP Q̄ (pin 2)		2nd NOR GATE: Tr2 (pin 6)
9	2nd NOR GATE (pin 4)		LED GREEN 2

TRUTH TABLE

	LEDs												
6	RED 1	1	1	1	0	0	0	0	1	1	1	0	0	0	0
4	YELLOW 1	0	0	0	1	0	0	0	1	0	0	0	1	0	0	0	1
7	GREEN 1	0	0	0	0	1	1	1	0	0	0	0	1	1	1	0
8	RED 2	0	0	0	0	1	1	1	1	0	0	0	0	1	1	1	1
4	YELLOW 2	0	0	0	1	0	0	0	1	0	0	0	1	0	0	0	1
9	GREEN 2	1	1	1	0	0	0	0	1	1	1	0	0	0	0
	STAGES →	1		2		3		4		1		2		3		4

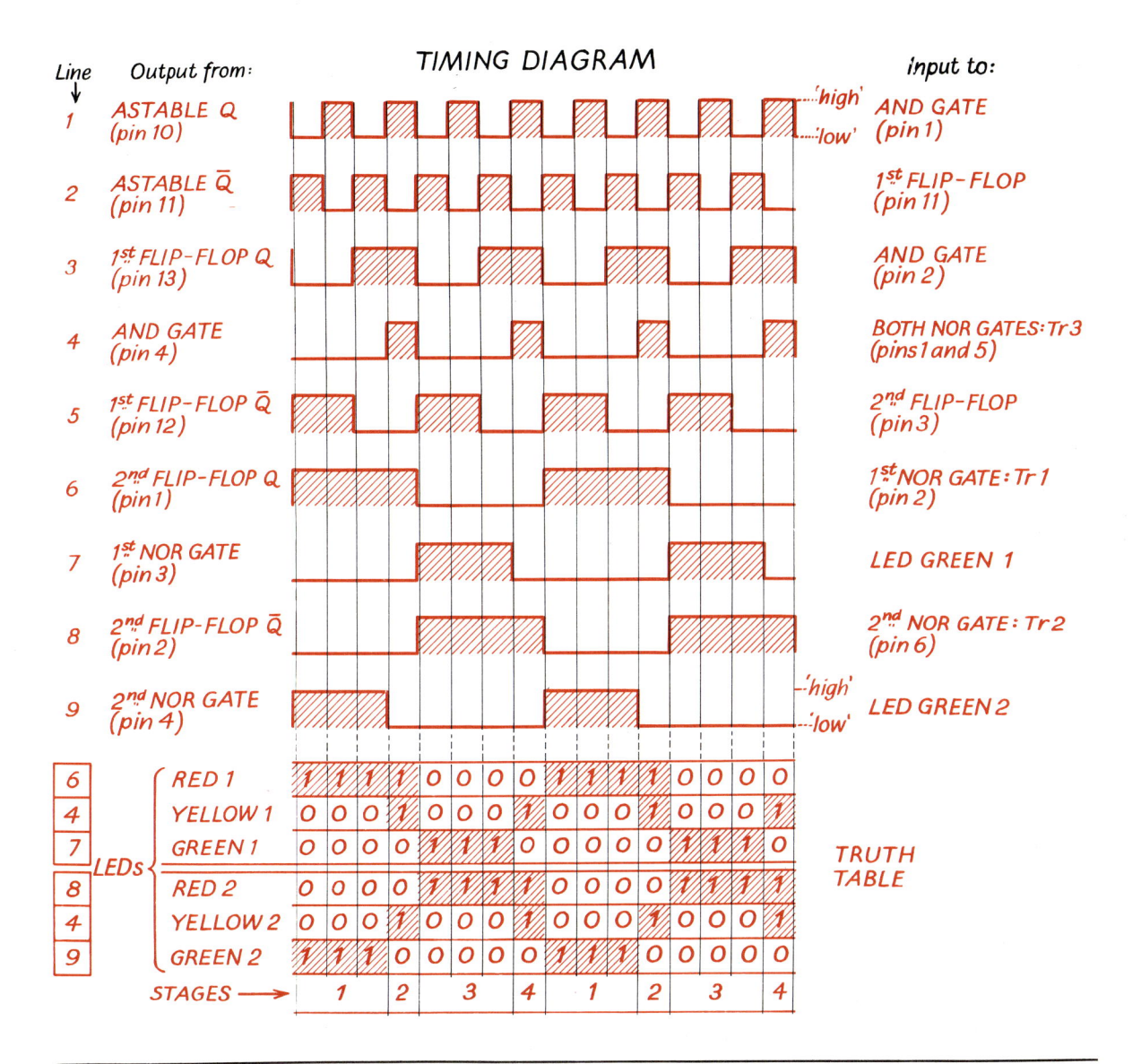

THINGS TO TRY OR THINK ABOUT

1 *Prediction and test.* Predict what will happen if you trigger the first flip-flop from the Q output of the astable rather than the Q̄ output by constructing a timing diagram like the one above. Check your prediction by altering the circuit.

2 In the system you have built the red and green LEDs are on alone for three times as long as the yellow LEDs. What would be the effect of using (*a*) one flip-flop, (*b*) three flip-flops, in the circuit instead of two?

39

4 Two-way traffic lights II

Two-way traffic signals in Britain have an all-red stage for both directions and require each complete cycle of operations to have eight stages. The correct timing sequence is achieved in this model by employing an astable to drive a four-bit binary counter in which only eight (of the sixteen available) output states are used.

The project illustrates how truth tables and timing diagrams aid the design of electronic systems, as you will see later.

WHAT YOU NEED

Astable IC (4047B); binary counter IC (4516B); quad 2-input NAND gate IC (4011B); two quad 2-input NOR gate ICs (4001B); four npn transistors (ZTX300); six LEDs (two red, two yellow, two green); resistors – six 680 Ω (blue grey brown), 2.2 MΩ (red red green); ceramic capacitor – 0.1 μF; 9 V battery; battery clip connector; two circuit boards; PVC-covered tinned copper wire 1/0.6 mm.

HERE IS THE CIRCUIT

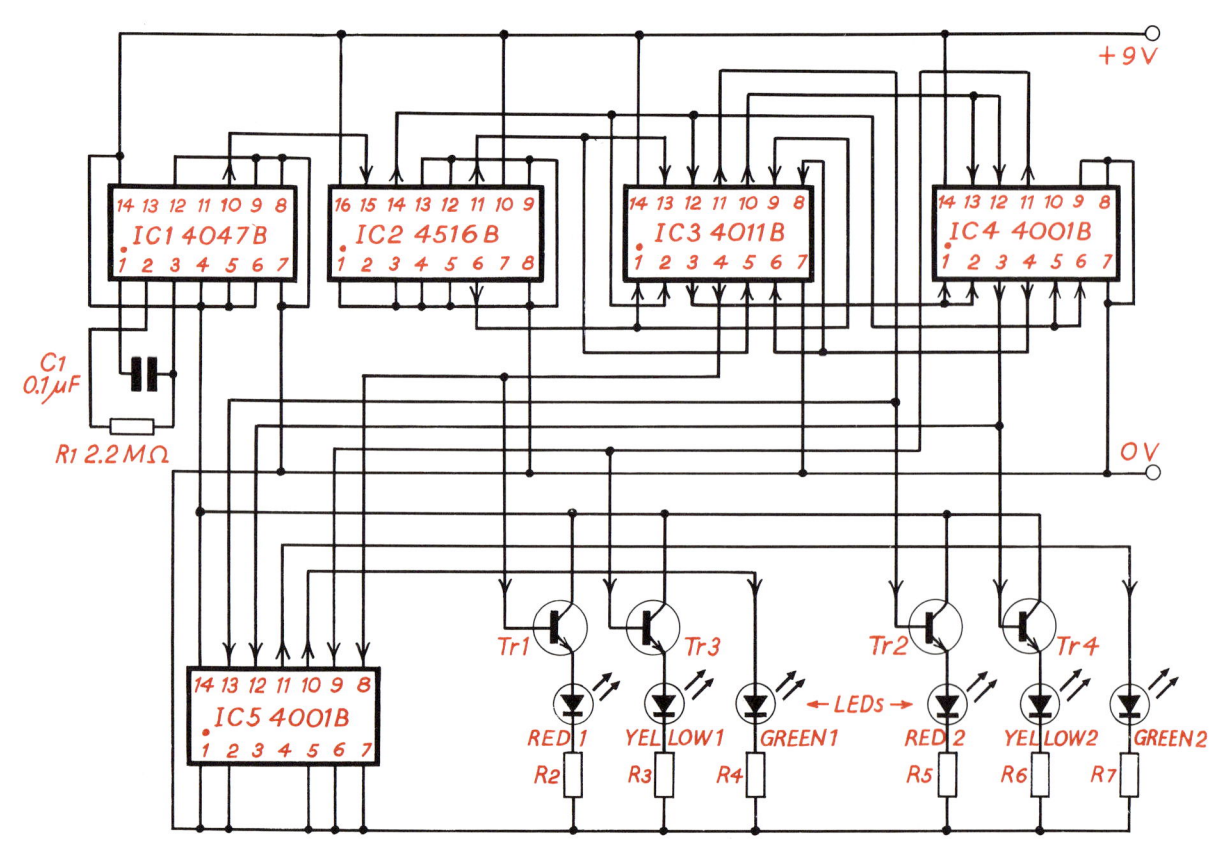

Tr1 to Tr4 ZTX300
R2 to R7 680 Ω

IC PIN CONNECTIONS: 4047B (p.10), 4516B (p.15), 4011B (p.8), 4001B (p.8)

HOW TO BUILD IT

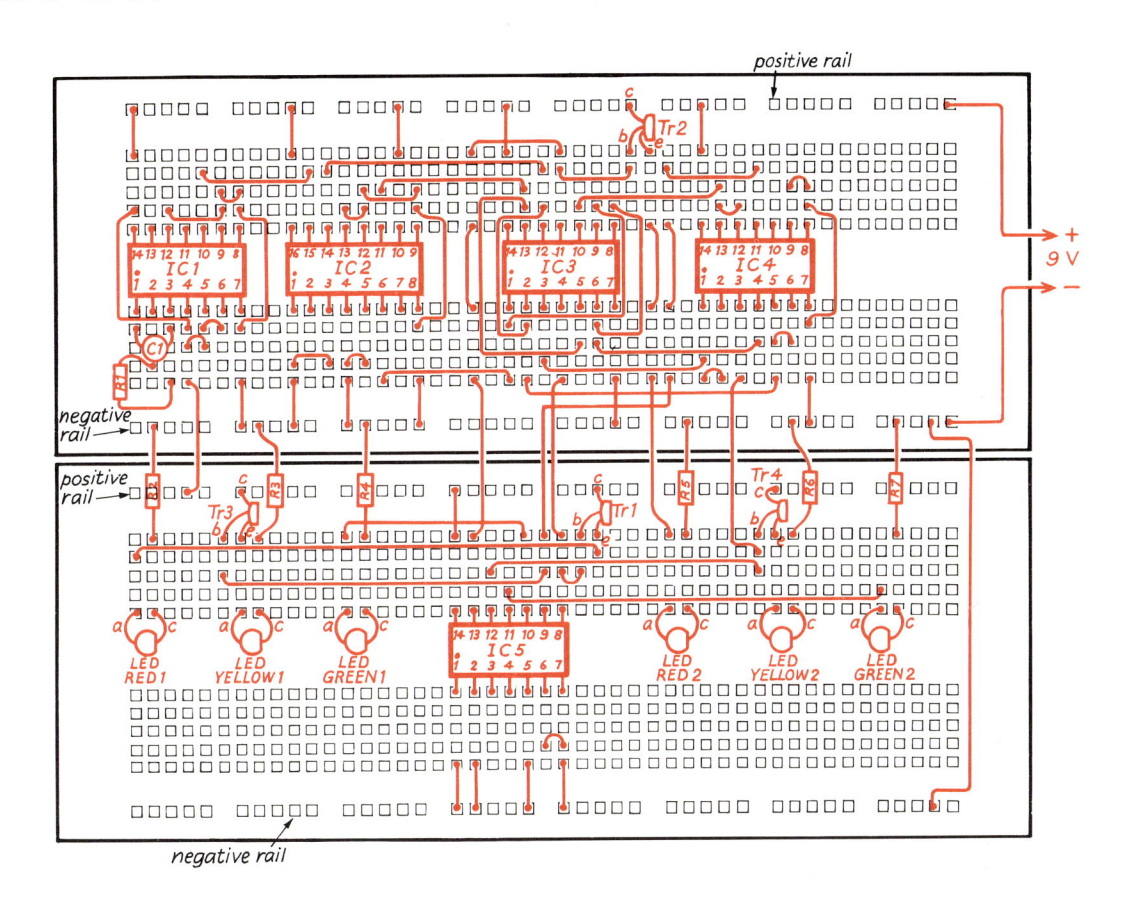

1 Couple two circuit boards together, side by side.
2 Identify pin 1 on the ICs from the small dot or notch at one end of the case. Carefully push each IC into the circuit board in the positions shown, taking care not to bend the pins in the process.
3 Insert wire links from each IC to the positive and negative rails and between other sockets, as shown.
4 Insert *R*1 to *R*7 and *C*1.
5 Identify the collector (c), base (b) and emitter (e) leads on the transistors. Insert them in the circuit board, as shown, making sure that the leads are not touching one another.
6 Insert the LEDs as shown, remembering that the cathode is next to the 'flat' at the bottom of the plastic case.
7 CHECK THE CIRCUIT CAREFULLY. 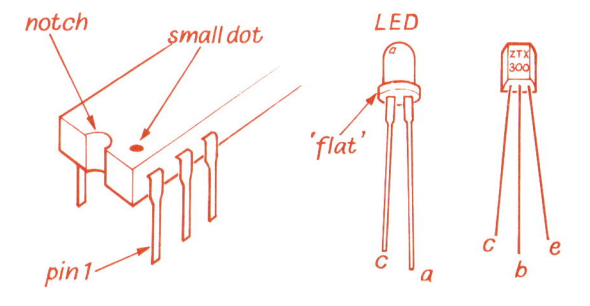
8 Connect the battery with the *correct polarity*. The LEDs should light in the order given in the truth table (page 43), where 1 represents a lit LED and 0 an unlit one. If any don't light when they should, they may be wrongly connected.

41

HOW IT WORKS

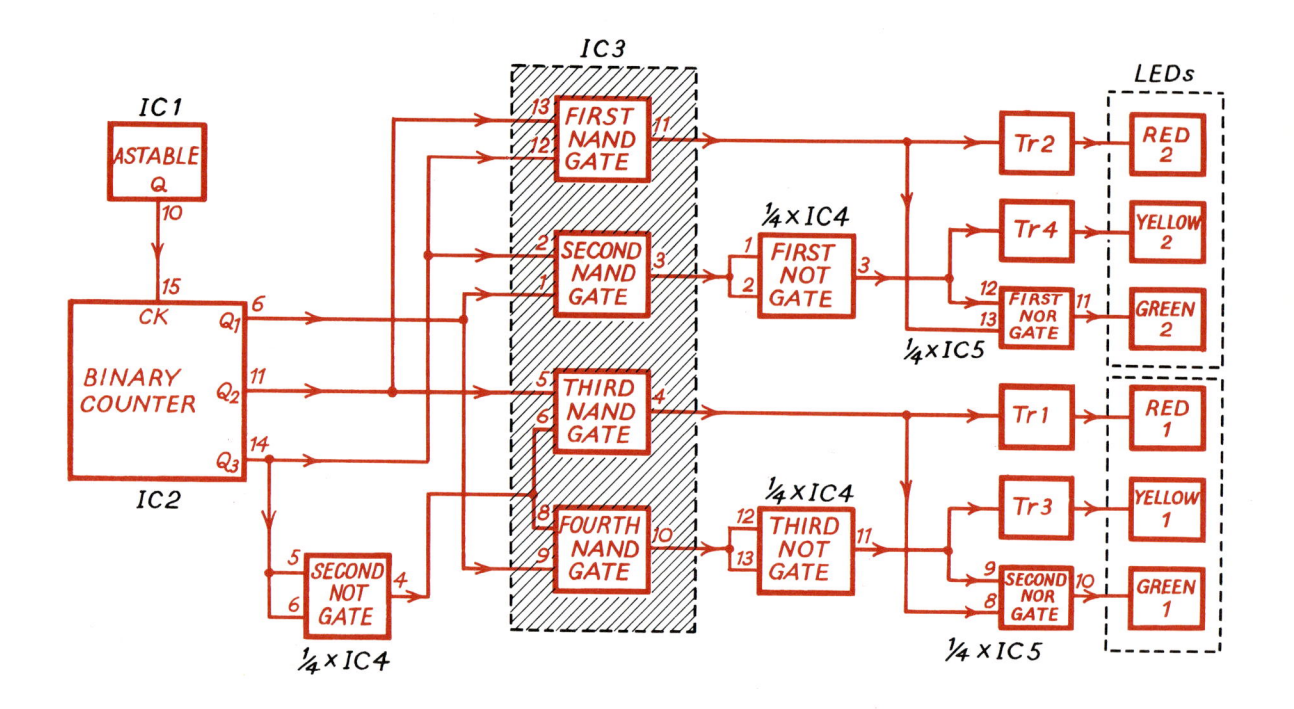

The block diagram is shown above and opposite is the timing diagram for the ASTABLE (clock) and the three least significant outputs Q_1, Q_2 and Q_3 (and its complement $\bar{Q}_3$) of the BINARY COUNTER which it feeds. The action of the circuit depends on the fact that the output of a NAND GATE is 'high' unless all its inputs are 'high' (page 7). From the truth table below the timing diagram we see that:

(i) RED 1 is always 'high' except during stages 3 and 4 of the 8-stage cycle of operations. None of the Q outputs on its own from the BINARY COUNTER gives the sequence of states required by this LED. Inspection of the timing diagram shows however that Q_2 and $\bar{Q}_3$ are both 'high' for stages 3 and 4 only, therefore if they supplied the inputs to a 2-input NAND GATE, the NAND GATE output would be 'low' during these stages – which is the desired lighting sequence. Q_2 and $\bar{Q}_3$ are thus used as the inputs to the THIRD NAND GATE and its output drives LED RED 1 via $Tr1$. $\bar{Q}_3$ is obtained by inverting Q_3 (using the SECOND NOT GATE) before it is applied to the NAND GATE. You should check these steps through from Q_2 and Q_3 to RED 1 on the block diagram.

(ii) YELLOW 1 is 'high' for stages 2 and 4. Inspection of the timing diagram shows that the Q_1 and $\bar{Q}_3$ outputs from the BINARY COUNTER are both 'high' then. If they supply the inputs to the FOURTH NAND GATE ($\bar{Q}_3$ being obtained from Q_3 as before) the output from this gate will be 'low' during stages 2 and 4. To make it 'high', the THIRD NOT GATE is connected before $Tr3$ and YELLOW 1 to do the inverting. Again follow these steps in the block diagram.

(iii) GREEN 1 is 'high' when neither RED 1 nor YELLOW 1 is 'high'. This suggests that GREEN 1 might be driven from a NOR GATE (the SECOND) having the same inputs as RED 1 and YELLOW 1 – since the output from a NOR GATE is 'high' only when both inputs are 'low' (page 7). The block diagram shows the connections required.

You should now be able to understand from the timing diagram and the truth table the

TIMING DIAGRAM

STAGE →	1	2	3	4	5	6	7	8	1
ASTABLE									
Q_1									
Q_2									
Q_3									
$\bar{Q}_3$									

output from: ASTABLE, Q_1, Q_2, Q_3, $\bar{Q}_3$

TRUTH TABLE

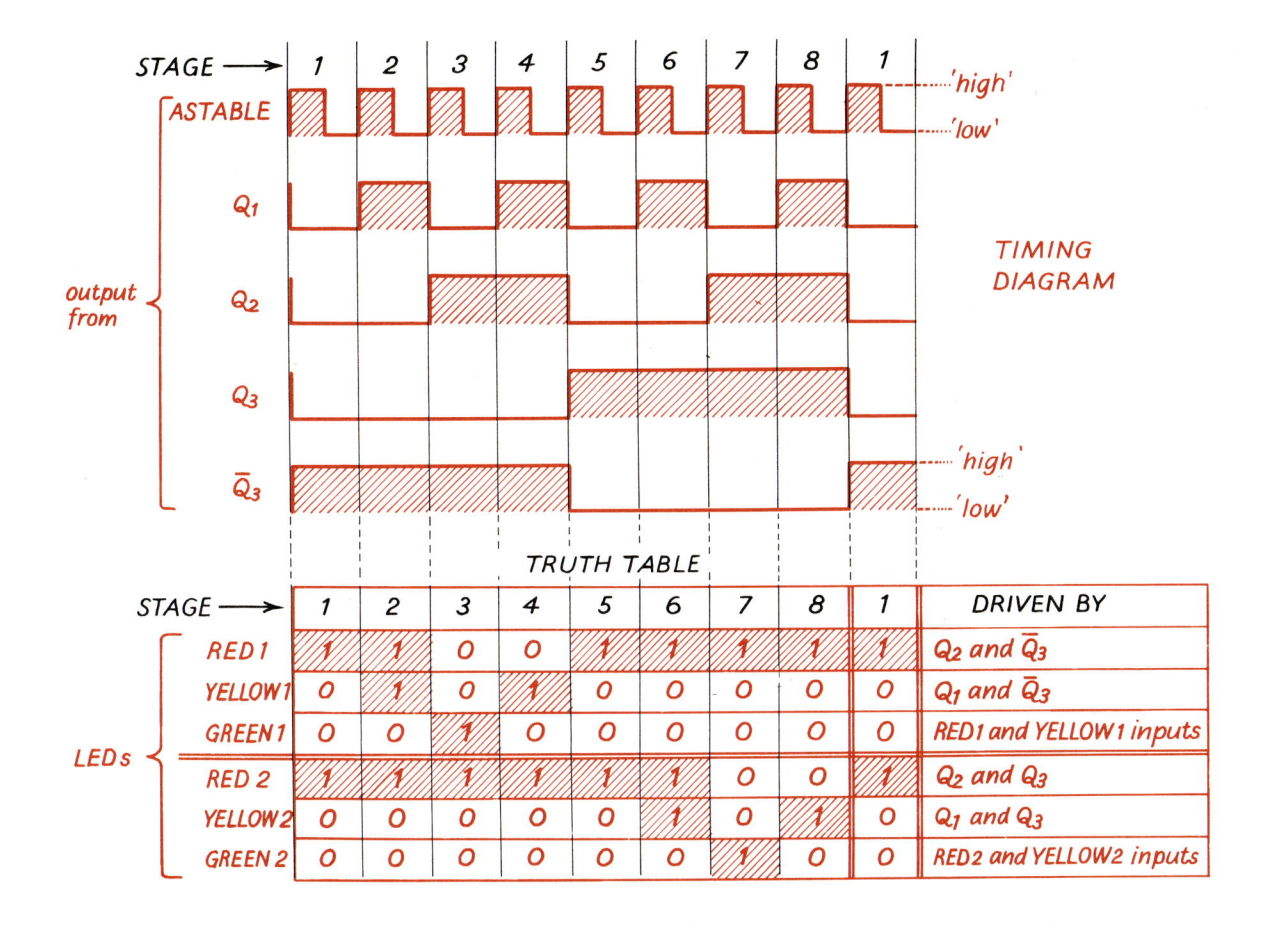

STAGE →	1	2	3	4	5	6	7	8	1	DRIVEN BY
RED 1	1	1	0	0	1	1	1	1	1	Q_2 and $\bar{Q}_3$
YELLOW 1	0	1	0	1	0	0	0	0	0	Q_1 and $\bar{Q}_3$
GREEN 1	0	0	1	0	0	0	0	0	0	RED1 and YELLOW1 inputs
RED 2	1	1	1	1	1	1	0	0	1	Q_2 and Q_3
YELLOW 2	0	0	0	0	0	1	0	1	0	Q_1 and Q_3
GREEN 2	0	0	0	0	0	0	1	0	0	RED2 and YELLOW2 inputs

slightly simpler circuit arrangements needed to light RED 2, YELLOW 2 and GREEN 2 in the correct sequence. RED 2 is driven by the FIRST NAND GATE with Q_2 and Q_3 as inputs and YELLOW 2 by the inverted output from the SECOND NAND GATE. GREEN 2 operates from the same inputs as RED 2 and YELLOW 2 via the FIRST NOR GATE.

Notes. 1. The three NOT gates are made by joining both inputs (to give single inputs) in three of the NOR gates in *IC*4 (page 8).
2. The frequency of the ASTABLE depends on the values of *R*1 and *C*1 (page 10).

THINGS TO TRY

Work out what you think will happen if output Q_1 from the BINARY COUNTER is disconnected. Put your predictions in a truth table then check them experimentally.

5 Pedestrian crossing signals

WHAT YOU NEED

Dual D flip-flop IC (4013B); dual astable IC (556); decade counter IC (4017B); quad 2-input NAND gate IC (4011B); two quad 2-input NOR gate ICs (4001B); astable IC (4047B); four npn transistors (ZTX300); five LEDs (two red, two green, one yellow); resistors – 100 Ω (brown black brown), five 680 Ω (blue grey brown), 4.7 kΩ (yellow violet red), 47 kΩ (yellow violet orange), 100 kΩ (brown black yellow), 220 kΩ (red red yellow), 1 MΩ (brown black green), 2.2 MΩ (red red green); ceramic capacitors – two 0.01 μF, 0.1 μF; electrolytic capacitors – two 1 μF; keyboard push switch; loudspeaker 2½ in, 25 to 80 Ω; 9 V battery; battery clip connector; two circuit boards; PVC-covered tinned copper wire 1/0.6 mm.

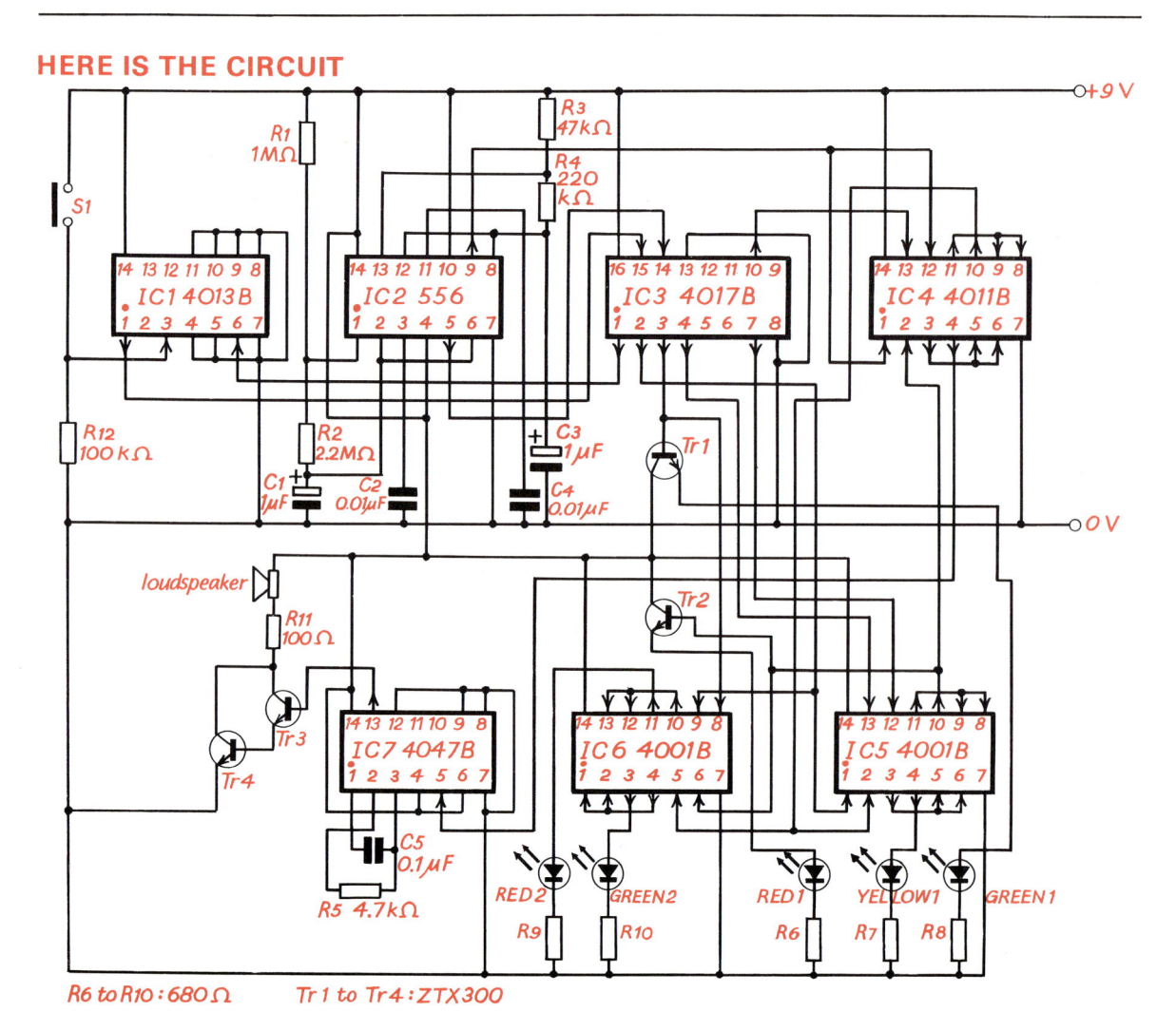

In this life-like model the signals are normally set at 'go' for the traffic and 'stop' for pedestrians. By pushing a switch you can 'stop' the traffic and produce the cycle of changes, including 'bleeps' and 'flashes', as in the real thing. The timing sequence is obtained using a decade counter.

HERE IS THE CIRCUIT

R6 to R10 : 680 Ω   Tr 1 to Tr 4 : ZTX300

IC PIN CONNECTIONS : 4013B (p.12), 556 (p.9), 4017B (p.15), 4011B (p.8), 4001B (p.8), 4047B (p.10)

HOW TO BUILD IT

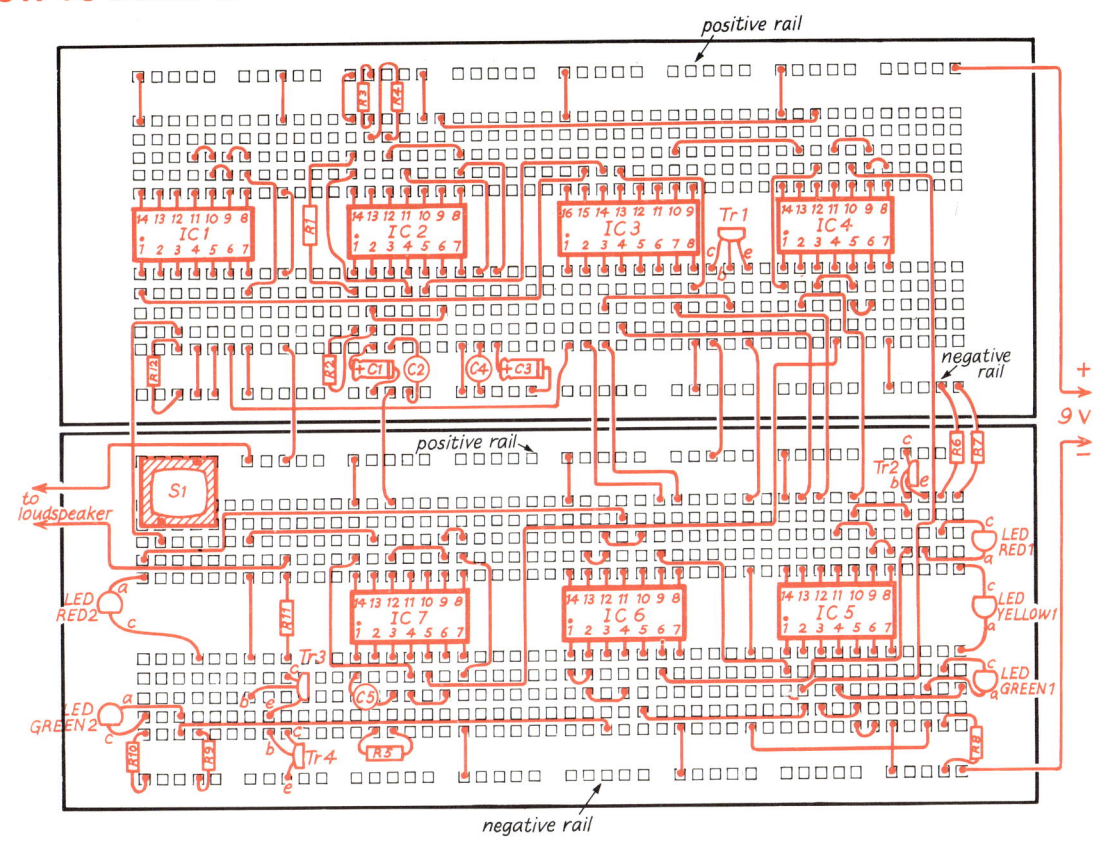

1. Couple two circuit boards together, side by side.
2. Identify pin 1 on the ICs from the small dot or notch at one end of the case. Carefully push each IC into the board in the position shown, taking care not to bend the pins in the process.
3. Insert wire links from each IC to the positive and negative rails and between other sockets, as shown.
4. Insert R1 to R12, C1 to C5 and S1. Be sure that C1 and C3 are connected the correct way round, the + end has a groove and the − end a black band (usually).
5. Identify the collector (c), base (b) and emitter (e) leads on the transistors. Insert them in the circuit board, as shown, making sure that the leads are not touching one another.
6. Insert the LEDs as shown, remembering that the cathode is next to the 'flat' at the bottom of the plastic case. Connect the loudspeaker.
7. CHECK THE CIRCUIT CAREFULLY. 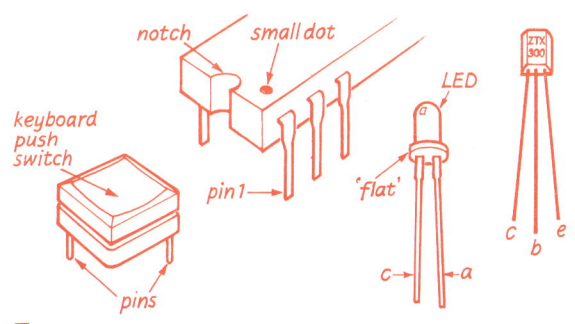
8. Connect the battery with the *correct polarity*. The LEDs should light in the order given in the truth table (page 46) where 1 represents a lit LED and 0 an unlit one. If any don't light when they should, they may be connected the wrong way round. During stage 3, there should be 'bleeps' from the loudspeaker. In stage 4, LEDs Yellow 1 and Green 2 should be flashing.

45

HOW IT WORKS

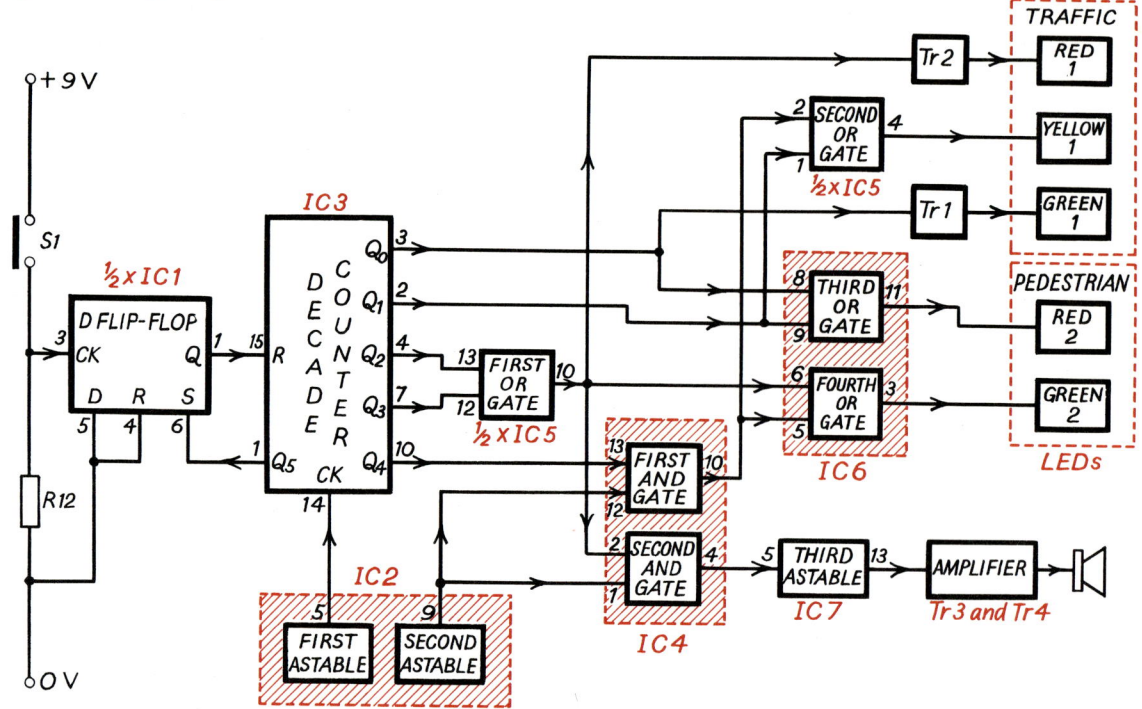

The block diagram shows that the output from the FIRST ASTABLE (pin 5) is applied to the 'clock' input CK (pin 14) of the DECADE COUNTER and drives it at a slow rate (determined by *R*1, *R*2 and *C*1, page 10). If 'reset' R (pin 15) on the counter is 'low', counting of the clock pulses from the astable occurs, i.e. outputs Q_0, Q_1, etc. go 'high' in turn (page 15). When Q_5 (pin 1) is 'high', it makes the 'set' input S (pin 6) on the D FLIP-FLOP go 'high' and so puts the Q output (pin 1) 'high' (i.e. the flip-flop operates in the *direct mode*, page 12). This makes 'reset' R (pin 15) on the counter go 'high', causing it to reset, i.e. Q_0 becomes 'high' and all other outputs go 'low', including Q_5. LED Green 1 is therefore alight (via *Tr*1) as is Red 2 because *one* of the inputs (pin 8) is 'high' to the THIRD OR GATE which drives it (page 7). This is the normal state of the system, i.e. 'go' for traffic and 'stop' for pedestrians.

Since Q_5 is now 'low' both R and S on the flip-flop are 'low', allowing it to operate in the *clocked mode*. Consequently when *S*1 is closed, the 'clock' input CK (pin 3) rises from 0 V (due to the connection via *R*12 to 0 V) to 9 V, and on the resulting rising edge (⎍) the 'low' state of the D input (pin 5) is transferred to the Q output, i.e. Q now goes 'low'. Counting can then start again.

Q_1 (pin 2) goes 'high' after Q_0, therefore Red 2 is kept 'high' by the THIRD OR GATE (pin 8)

TRUTH TABLE

	STAGE →	1	2	3	4	1
TRAFFIC LEDs	RED 1	0	0	1 + bleeps	0	0
	YELLOW 1	0	1	0	flashes	0
	GREEN 1	1	0	0	0	1
PEDESTRIAN LEDs	RED 2	1	1	0	0	1
	GREEN 2	0	0	1 + bleeps	flashes	0

and the SECOND OR GATE (pin 1) drives Yellow 1 'high'. The other LEDs are unlit since the other outputs are 'low'. This is stage 2 in the sequence.

Q_2 (pin 4) and Q_3 (pin 7) provide the inputs to the FIRST OR GATE, so that when either is 'high', the output (pin 10) from the gate is 'high', thereby making stage 3 last twice as long as any other (giving pedestrians 'time to cross the road'). Red 1 is now alight (via $Tr2$), as is Green 2 because one of the inputs (pin 6) to the FOURTH OR GATE is 'high'. To obtain the 'bleeps' for this stage the output from the FIRST OR GATE is also supplied to one input of the SECOND AND GATE (pin 2), the second input (pin 1) coming from the SECOND ASTABLE which produces 'faster' pulses (due to $R3$, $R4$ and $C3$) than those from the FIRST ASTABLE. The FIRST OR GATE provides a 'long' pulse (when Q_2 or Q_3 is 'high') which 'opens' the SECOND AND GATE to allow about twenty 'shorter' pulses from the SECOND ASTABLE to pass into the THIRD ASTABLE. The latter 'fills' each pulse in with even 'shorter' pulses (determined by $R5$ and $C5$) because the THIRD ASTABLE is only 'enabled' (pin 5) when the output from the SECOND AND GATE is 'high'. The 'fast' pulses from the THIRD ASTABLE are amplified by $Tr3$ and $Tr4$ to give an audible note in the loudspeaker.

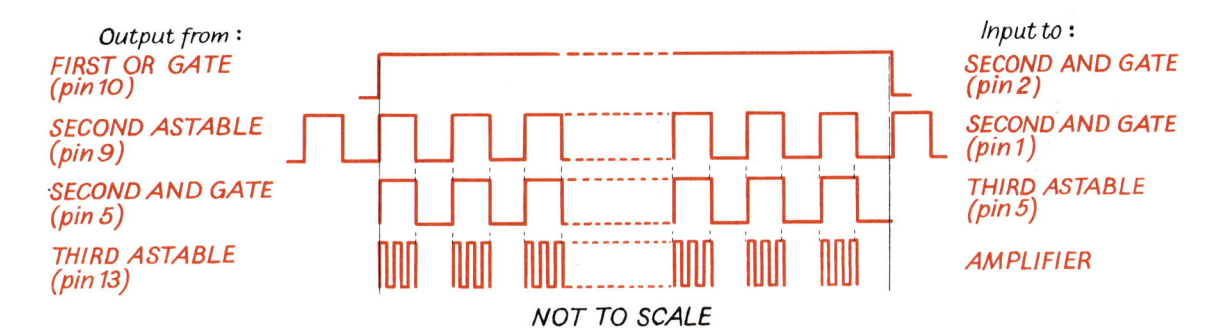

In stage 4, Q_4 (pin 10) goes 'high' and opens the FIRST AND GATE to the SECOND ASTABLE, thereby causing the output from the gate (pin 10) to switch several times a second between 'high' and 'low'. 'Flashing' of Green 2 occurs via the FOURTH OR GATE and also of Yellow 1 via the SECOND OR GATE.

When Q_5 goes 'high', the counter resets to the 'normal' state until $S1$ is pressed again. The whole sequence takes about 15 seconds.

Note. Each AND gate is formed by combining two NAND gates and each OR gate from two NOR gates.

THINGS TO TRY

1 Predict and then check what happens if you remove the THIRD ASTABLE IC7 from the circuit and connect the output from the SECOND AND GATE IC4 (pin 4) to the AMPLIFIER (base of $Tr3$).

2 By referring to the truth table for the D FLIP-FLOP (page 12) work out if the system still functions when *all* the following changes are made:

(i) R (pin 15) on the COUNTER is disconnected from Q (pin 1) on the FLIP-FLOP and joined to $\bar{Q}$ (pin 2) on the FLIP-FLOP,

(ii) R (pin 4) on the FLIP-FLOP is disconnected from 0 V,

(iii) S (pin 6) on the FLIP-FLOP is disconnected from Q_5 (pin 1) on the COUNTER,

(iv) S (pin 6) is connected to 0 V,

(v) R (pin 4) on the FLIP-FLOP is connected to Q_5 (pin 1) on the COUNTER and

(vi) D (pin 5) is disconnected from 0 V and joined to +9 V.

Check your conclusions in practice.

6 Electronic fruit machine

WHAT YOU NEED

Astable IC (4047B); binary counter IC (4516B); quad 2-input NAND gate IC (4011B); dual 4-input NOR gate IC (4002B); dual astable IC (556); five npn transistors (ZTX300); four LEDs; keyboard push switch; resistors – four 680 Ω (blue grey brown), 1 kΩ (brown black red), 4.7 kΩ (yellow violet red), two 10 kΩ (brown black orange), three 100 kΩ (brown black yellow), 470 kΩ (yellow violet yellow); ceramic capacitors – three 0.01 μF, 0.1 μF; electrolytic capacitors – 1 μF, 4.7 μF; loudspeaker 2½ in, 25 to 80 Ω; 9 V battery; battery clip connector; two circuit boards; PVC-covered tinned copper wire 1/0.6 mm.

In this electronic version of a fruit machine you 'hit the jackpot' if four flashing lights all stay on when you press a switch. Your success will be announced, not unfortunately by an avalanche of coins, but by an ear-splitting wail from the 'machine'.

HERE IS THE CIRCUIT

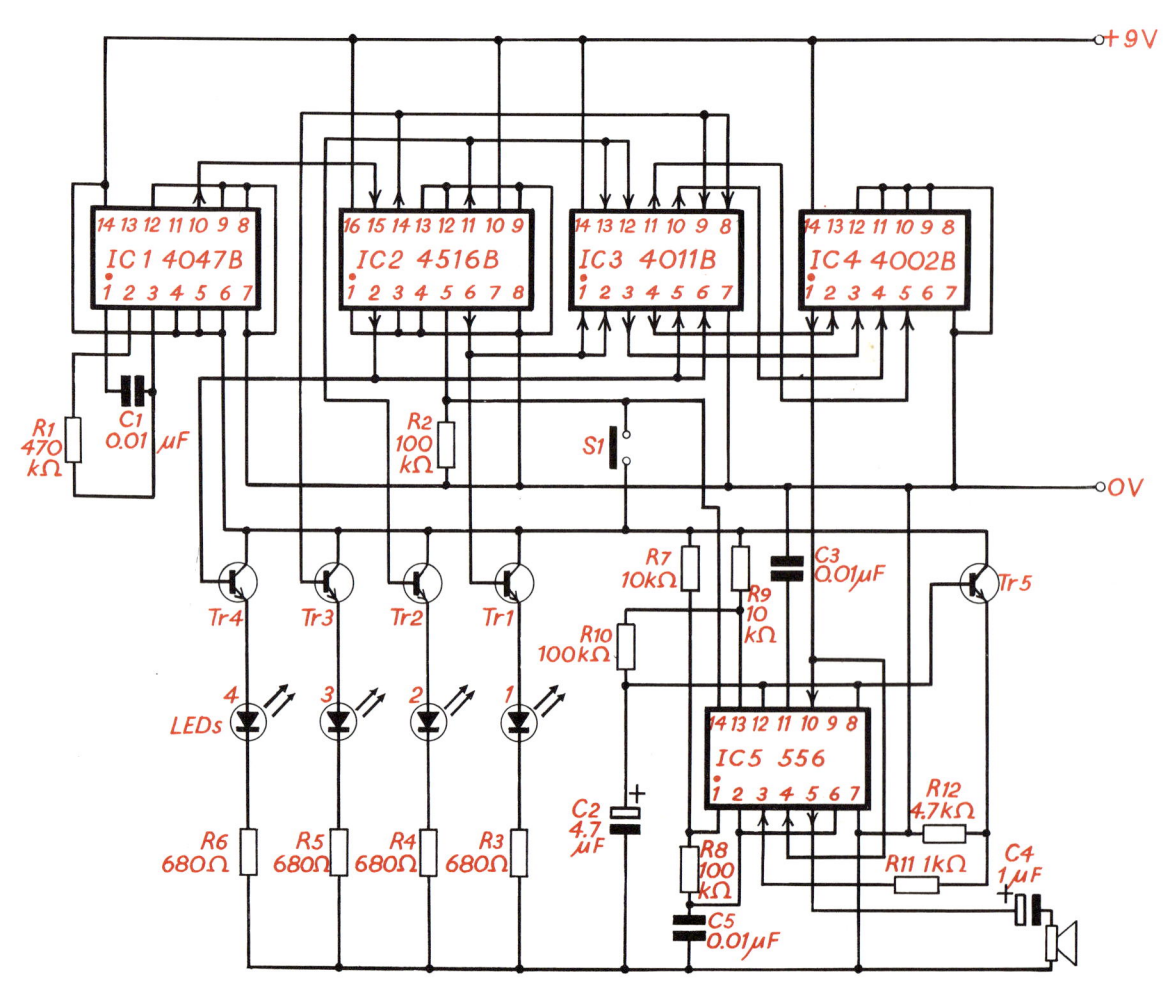

IC PIN CONNECTIONS: 4047(p.10), 4516(p.15), 4011B(p.8), 4002B(p.8), 556(p.9)

HOW TO BUILD IT

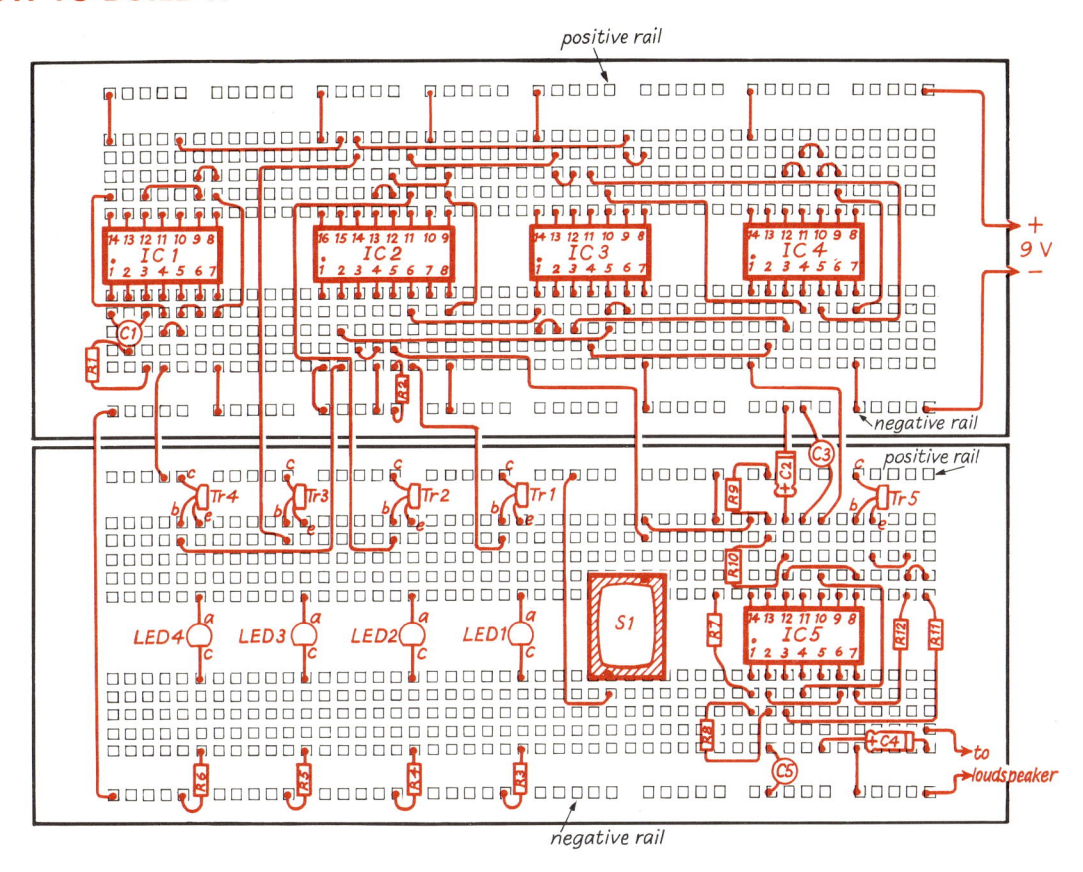

1. Couple two circuit boards together, side by side.
2. Identify pin 1 on the ICs from the small dot or notch at one end of the case. Carefully push each IC into the board in the position shown, taking care not to bend the pins.
3. Insert wire links from each IC to the positive and negative rails and between other sockets, as shown.
4. Insert R1 to R12, C1 to C5 and S1. Be sure that C2 and C4 are connected the correct way round, the + end has a groove and the − end a black band (usually).
5. Identify the collector (c), base (b) and emitter (e) leads on the transistors. Insert them in the circuit board, as shown, making sure that the leads are not touching one another.
6. Insert the LEDs as shown, remembering that the cathode is next to the 'flat' at the bottom of the plastic case. Connect the loudspeaker.
7. CHECK THE CIRCUIT CAREFULLY. 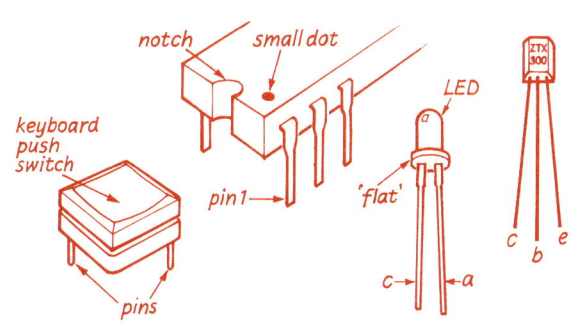
8. Connect the battery with the *correct polarity*. The LEDs should all start flashing, the one on the extreme right at a much faster rate (8 times) than the one on the extreme left. If any do not, they may be connected the wrong way.

When S1 is pressed, the flashing stops, leaving some, all or none of the LEDs alight. If all stay alight, the 'jackpot' has been won and a 'wail' should be emitted from the loudspeaker. On releasing S1 the flashing starts again.

49

HOW IT WORKS

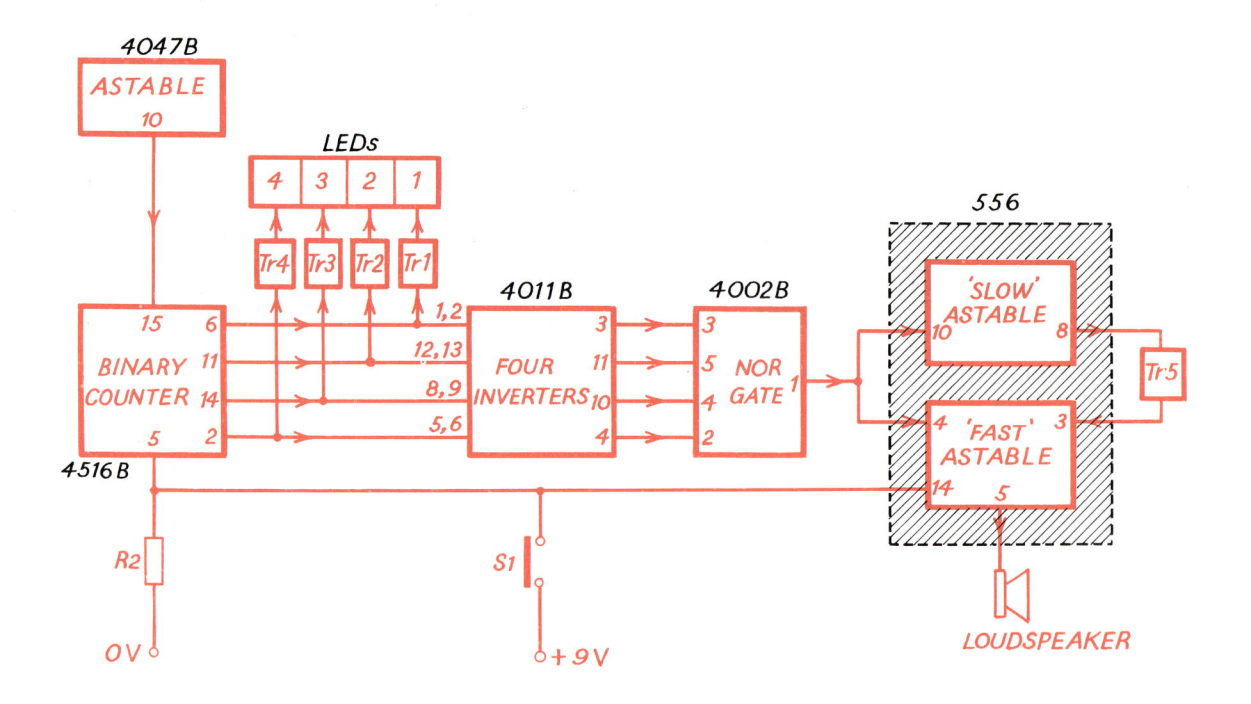

Pulses from the Q output (pin 10) of the ASTABLE are applied to the 'clock input' CK (pin 15) of the BINARY COUNTER at a rate determined by R1 and C1 (page 10). The pulses are counted and displayed in binary code by the four LEDs which are driven (via transistors) by the four outputs (pins 6, 11, 14 and 2) of the BINARY COUNTER. The count goes very quickly from 0 (all LEDs off) through to 15 (all LEDs on) again and again. However if S1 is pressed, 'carry in' CI (pin 5) on the BINARY COUNTER goes from 'low' (because of its connection via R2 to 0 V) to 'high' (i.e. 9 V) and this stops the counter (page 14) to give a static LED display in which all, some or no LEDs are alight.

The four outputs from the BINARY COUNTER are also inverted (i.e. 'high' (1) becomes 'low' (0) and vice versa) by the quad 2-input NAND GATE which is connected as FOUR INVERTERS. Therefore, when *all* the counter outputs are 'high', the outputs (pins 3, 11, 10 and 4) from the FOUR INVERTERS are *all* 'low' and, being the inputs (pins 3, 5, 4 and 2) to the 4-input NOR GATE, cause its output (pin 1) to go 'high' (page 7). For other input combinations to the NOR GATE the output is 'low'.

The NOR GATE output is applied to the 'resets' (pins 10 and 4) on both the 'SLOW' and 'FAST' ASTABLES. Hence, provided S1 is pressed (on), so applying 9 V to both ASTABLES, the latter operate when the NOR GATE output is 'high', i.e. all four inputs to the INVERTERS are 'high'. The 'SLOW' and 'FAST' ASTABLES produce a wailing sound as follows.

Sawtooth-shaped pulses occur across C2 in the 'SLOW' ASTABLE (due to the charge-discharge action of a capacitor) and are fed (pin 8) to the base of Tr5 and then via R11 to 'control voltage' (pin 3) on the 'FAST' ASTABLE. Fre-

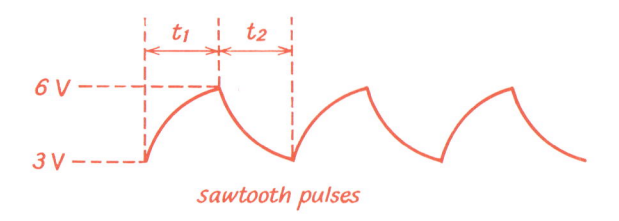

sawtooth pulses

quency modulation occurs (page 10), i.e. the control voltage on the 'FAST' ASTABLE varies *slowly* causing its output voltage (pin 5) frequency to rise slowly from a low value to a high value in time t_1 and then to fall slowly to a low value in time t_2 (where $t_1 + t_2$ is approximately 1 second).

The average value of the frequency about which the note rises and falls is 700 Hz (determined by $R7$, $R8$ and $C5$). $Tr5$ acts as an 'emitter follower' and ensures efficient transfer of the sawtooth pulses from the 'SLOW' to the 'FAST' ASTABLE.

THINGS TO TRY

1 *Action in slow motion.* Change $C1$ from 0.01 µF to 0.1 µF. You will now be able to follow the LEDs counting from 0 to 15; the least significant bit being given by LED 1 on the extreme right.

2 *Prediction and test.* Predict what will happen if pin 14 on IC5 is connected permanently to 9 V instead of to $S1$. Check your prediction by altering the circuit, first with $C1$ as 0.1 µF and then as 0.01 µF.

7 Computer space invaders

Whether you win or lose this 'space war' game, you should at least learn something about *memories* and *comparators* and also become expert at counting in binary – certainly up to 15! The circuit represents electronically a fleet of sixteen earth-orbiting space ships which are under your command and are being attacked by an 'alien being' from another world. 'Hits' will be both seen and heard and the total number recorded automatically in binary – or, if you prefer, in decimal.

WHAT YOU NEED

16-word 4-bit RAM IC (40114B); quad 2-input NAND gate IC (4011B); 4-bit comparator IC (4585B); binary counter IC (4516B); dual astable IC (556); four npn transistors (ZTX300); four LEDs; two d.i.l. 4-SPST switches; five keyboard push switches; slide switch SPDT; resistors – four 680 Ω (blue grey brown), 1 kΩ (brown black red), three 10 kΩ (brown black orange), 27 kΩ (red violet orange), fourteen 100 kΩ (brown black yellow); ceramic capacitors – two 0.01 μF; electrolytic capacitors – two 1 μF; loudspeaker 2½ in, 25 to 80 Ω; 9 V battery; battery clip connector; two circuit boards; PVC-covered tinned copper wire 1/0.6 mm.

HERE IS THE CIRCUIT

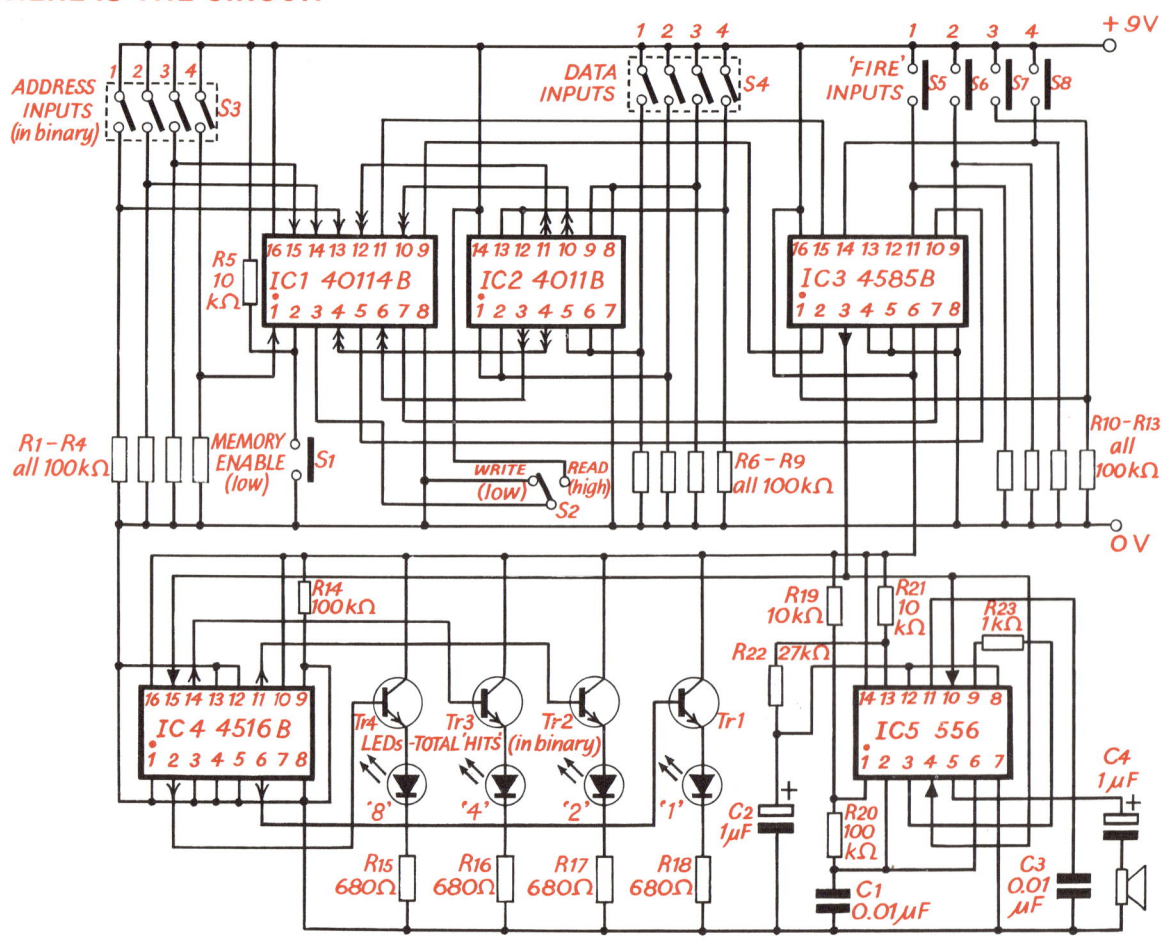

IC PIN CONNECTIONS: 40114B (p.18); 4011B (p.8), 4585B (p.20), 4516B (p.15), 556 (p.9)

HOW TO BUILD IT

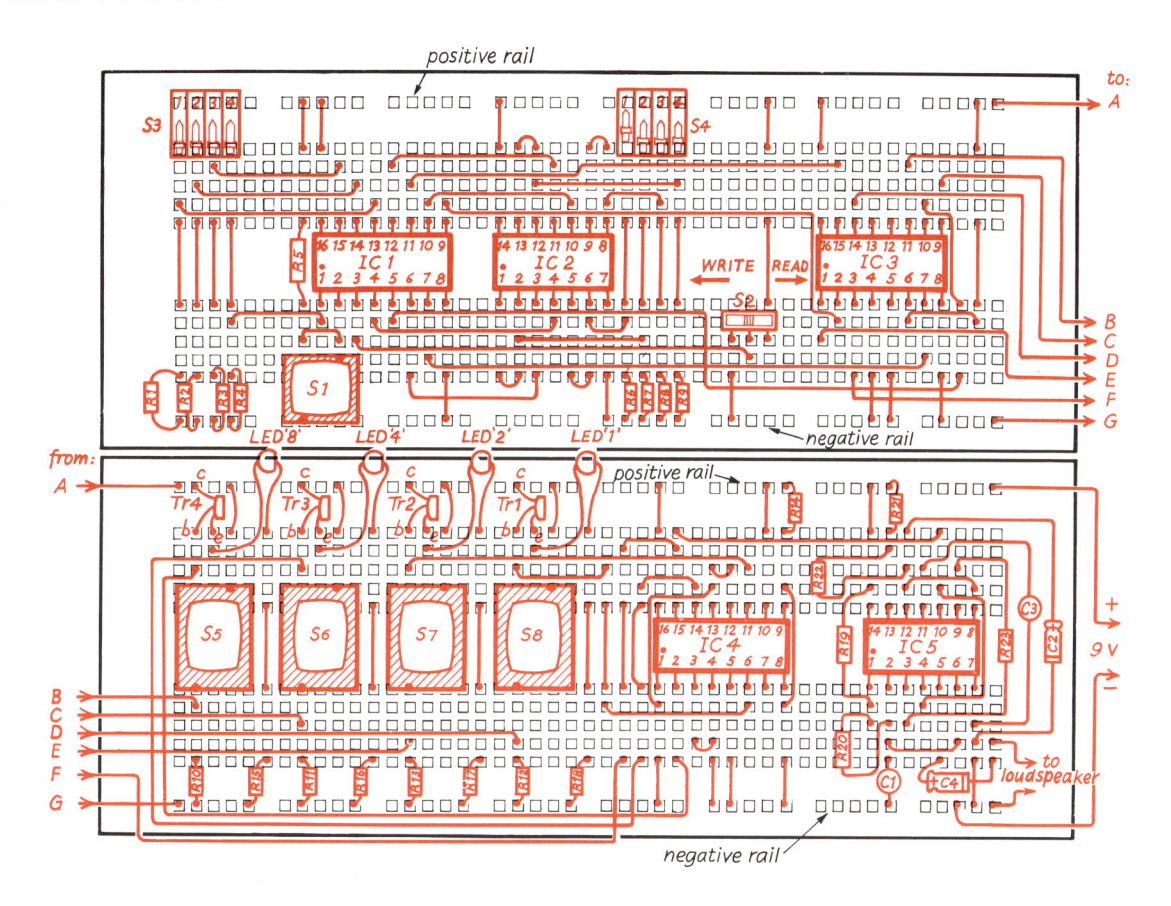

1. Couple two circuit boards together, end to end.
2. Identify pin 1 on the ICs from the small dot or notch at one end of the case. Carefully push each IC into the board in the position shown, taking care not to bend the pins.
3. Insert wire links from each IC to the positive and negative rails and between other sockets, as shown.
4. Insert R1 to R23, C1 to C4 and S1 to S8. Be sure that C2 and C4 are connected the correct way round, the + end has a groove and the − end a black band (usually).
5. Identify the collector (c), base (b) and emitter (e) leads on the transistors. Insert them in the circuit board, as shown, making sure that the leads are not touching one another.
6. Insert the LEDs as shown, remembering that the cathode is next to the 'flat' at the bottom of the plastic case. Connect the loudspeaker.
7. CHECK THE CIRCUIT CAREFULLY. 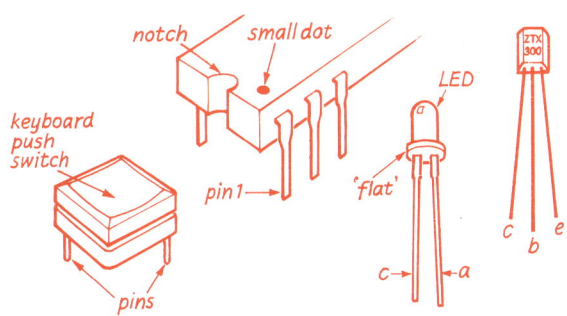
8. Connect the battery with the *correct polarity*. If any of the LEDs light, disconnect pin 9 on IC4 from 0 V for a second or so, thereby letting it go 'high' and resetting the counter to zero. *To test the circuit*, on S4, switch '1' on (i.e. up) and '2', '3' and '4' off (i.e. down), switch S2 to 'write' (i.e. left), press and release S1. Now switch S2 to 'read' (i.e. right), press S1 and S5 *at the same time*; LED '1' should light and

53

stay alight. There should also be a 'bleep' from the loudspeaker. *Keep S1 pressed* and check that pressing S6, S7 or S8 has no effect but that if S5 is pressed fifteen times more (with S1 still pressed) the LEDs record the total in binary at each stage (the right LED giving the least significant bit). If an LED does not light it could be the wrong way round.

You are now ready to go into 'battle'.

HOW TO PLAY 'COMPUTER SPACE INVADERS'

Two people can play in turn the roles of 'defender' and 'invader' to see who makes the most 'hits' with, say, sixteen 'shots'. Alternatively, you can take on both roles yourself if you 'forget' where you have located your space ships.

There are sixteen *orbits*, i.e. addresses in the memory, each identified by a four-bit binary number. Every orbit contains four space *stations* in only one of which does the 'defender' put a space *ship*. This is simulated by storing as data in each address, a four-bit number consisting of three '0's and one '1' (which represents a space ship). The table gives examples of how the switches in S3 and S4 *would* be set for the orbits, and *might* be set for the stations, respectively when the 'defender' is arranging his fleet. For instance, for orbit number 0, all four switches in S3 are off (i.e. down ↓) and if the second switch in S4 is on (i.e. up ↑) and the other three are off, then the space ship in that orbit occupies station number 2. The data is written into each address in turn (and kept secret) by first setting up S3 and S4 as described, then pressing S1 for a jiffy when S2 is on 'write' (i.e. to the left).

When all sixteen space ships are in position

Decimal	Binary	S3 positions 1	2	3	4	Station number	S4 positions 1	2	3	4
0	0000	↓	↓	↓	↓	2	↓	↑	↓	↓
1	0001	↓	↓	↓	↑	3	↓	↓	↑	↓
2	0010	↓	↓	↑	↓	2	↓	↑	↓	↓
3	0011	↓	↓	↑	↑	4	↓	↓	↓	↑
4	0100	↓	↑	↓	↓	1	↑	↓	↓	↓
5	0101	↓	↑	↓	↑	1	↑	↓	↓	↓
6	0110	↓	↑	↑	↓	3	↓	↓	↑	↓
7	0111	↓	↑	↑	↑	4	↓	↓	↓	↑
8	1000	↑	↓	↓	↓	2	↓	↑	↓	↓
9	1001	↑	↓	↓	↑	2	↓	↑	↓	↓
10	1010	↑	↓	↑	↓	1	↑	↓	↓	↓
11	1011	↑	↓	↑	↑	3	↓	↓	↑	↓
12	1100	↑	↑	↓	↓	2	↓	↑	↓	↓
13	1101	↑	↑	↓	↑	4	↓	↓	↓	↑
14	1110	↑	↑	↑	↓	1	↑	↓	↓	↓
15	1111	↑	↑	↑	↑	3	↓	↓	↑	↓

▨ = up = switch on = input '1'   ↓ = down = switch off = input '0'

battle can commence. First, the 'defender' switches S2 to 'read' (i.e. to the right) and then he sets the switches in S3 for orbit number 0. Next, with S1 pressed, he is ready for the 'invader' to 'fire' one shot by pressing *one* of S5, S6, S7 or S8. The shot will be aimed at station number 1 in orbit number 0 if S5 is pressed, at station number 2 if S6 is pressed and so on. In the example given in the table for orbit number 0, a 'hit' would be recorded if S6 were pressed.

Each orbit is 'attacked' in the same way, the 'defender' setting up the orbits one at a time and keeping S1 pressed (and S2 on 'read') when the 'invader' fires. After sixteen shots the total number of 'hits' is shown in binary on the LEDs (the lsb on the right).

The 'defender' and 'invader' then change roles, the new 'defender' altering the disposition of the space ships as he thinks fit.

If you wished you could have different rules. For example, you might let the 'invader' have as many shots as he needed to completely destroy your fleet – instead of just one shot per orbit. The game could be made more difficult for the 'invader' if the 'defender' distributed his sixteen space ships more randomly, i.e. not necessarily one per orbit. No doubt you can think of other variations (see also *Things to try* 2).

HOW IT WORKS

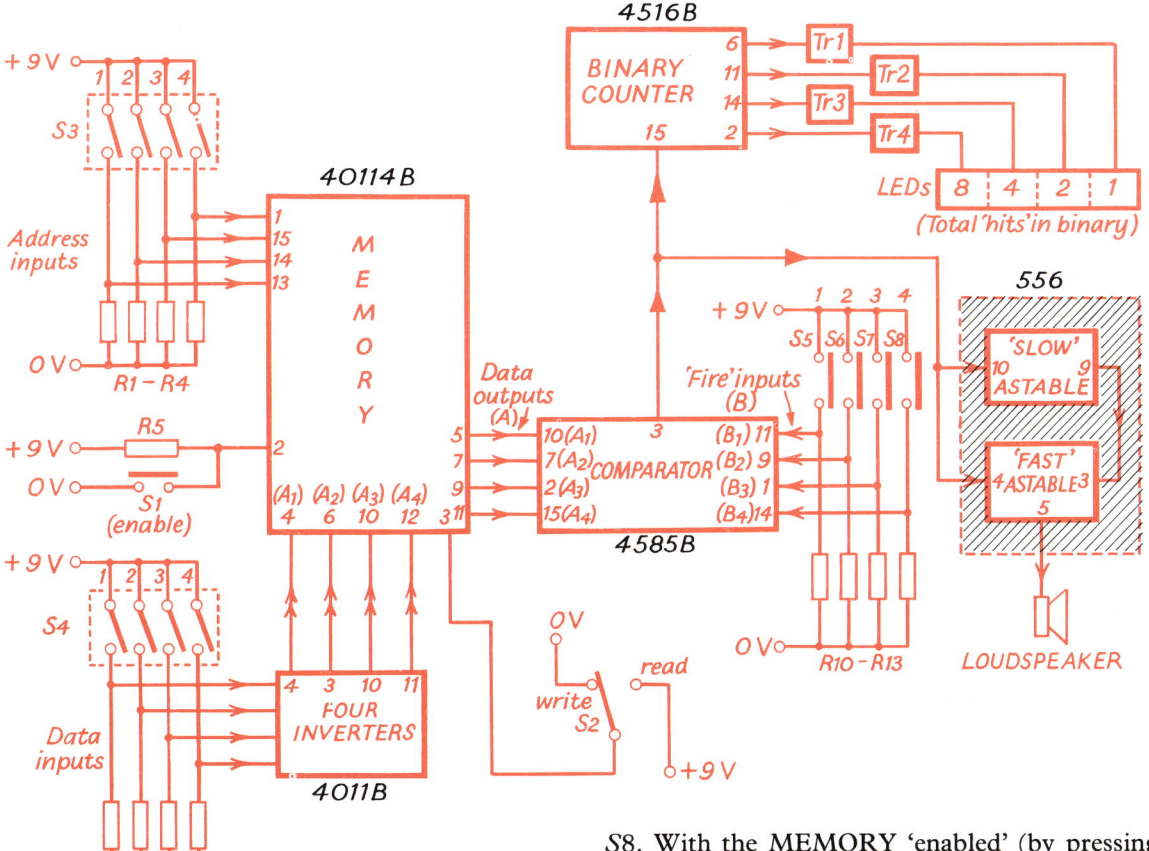

Two four-bit binary numbers A and B, are fed into the COMPARATOR, A from the MEMORY and B from the 'FIRE' switches S5, S6, S7 and S8. With the MEMORY 'enabled' (by pressing S1) and set to 'read' (by having S2 to the right), the COMPARATOR output $Q_{A=B}$ (pin 3) goes 'high' if A and B are *identical* and, being connected to the 'clock input' CK (pin 15) on the BINARY COUNTER, the resulting rising edge causes the count to advance by 1 (page 14) – as

55

indicated by the LEDs. The COMPARATOR $Q_{A=B}$ output is also applied to the 'resets' on both ASTABLES (pins 4 and 10) and allows them to produce a two-tone bleep in the loudspeaker (as explained in Project 2, page 34) when it goes 'high'.

Normally all the B inputs to the COMPARATOR are 'low' (0) due to their connections to 0 V via R10 to R13 but if any one of S5 to S8 is pressed, the corresponding B input goes 'high' (1) by being connected to 9 V. For example if S6 is pressed, $B_2 = 1$ and $B_1 = B_3 = B_4 = 0$.

The A inputs to the COMPARATOR are controlled by the settings of the four data input switches in S4. Any switch which is off, gives a 'low' (0) data input due to the connection to 0 V via R6, R7, R8 or R9; if a switch is on, the data input is connected to 9 V and goes 'high' (1). The *complements* of the data inputs would normally appear at the data outputs (pins 5, 7, 9 and 11) on the MEMORY but by inverting each data input (i.e. making 0's into 1's and vice versa) before it is applied to the MEMORY (using the FOUR INVERTERS or NOT GATES in the form of one-input NAND GATES, page 8), the *true* data outputs are obtained (i.e. a 1 input now gives a 1 output) and act as the A inputs to the COMPARATOR. For example, if switch 2 in S4 is on, $A_2 = 1$ and $A_1 = A_3 = A_4 = 0$. As a result, if the B input is as described in the previous paragraph (i.e. $B_2 = 1$ and $B_1 = B_3 = B_4 = 0$), the COMPARATOR output $Q_{A=B}$ goes 'high' and a 'hit' is recorded since A and B are equal binary numbers.

When the four switches in S3 are off, all address inputs are 'low' (0) due to their connections to 0 V via R1, R2, R3 or R4 but if any one is switched on, that input rises to 9 V and goes 'high' (1). The sixteen addresses in the MEMORY can thus be selected.

'Memory enable' ME (pin 2) is normally 'high' via R5 but it goes 'low' and allows the MEMORY to operate (i.e. 'write' or 'read') when S1 is pushed and connects it to 0 V. When 'write enable' WE (pin 3) is 'low', data can be 'written' into the MEMORY and when 'high', it can be 'read' out – the two-way switch S2 controls this action. Data 'written' into the MEMORY is lost (forgotten) almost as soon as the battery is disconnected.

THINGS TO TRY

1 *Decimal counting.* The total number of 'hits' can be recorded in decimal rather than in binary if the binary counter and four transistor-driven LEDs are replaced by a BCD counter (page 15), a BCD decoder-driver (page 22) and a 7-segment LED display (page 23).

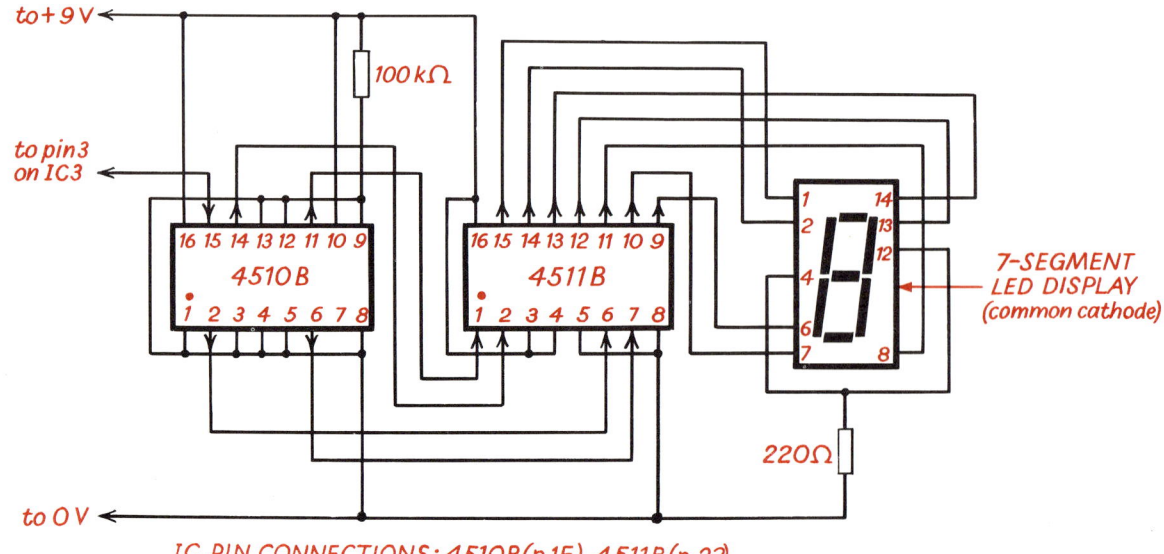

The circuit is shown opposite and will involve some rearrangement of components on the boards. The $Q_{A=B}$ output (pin 3) on the comparator now goes to the 'clock input' CK (pin 15) on the BCD counter. Connect the circuit and try it out. If the total 'hits' exceed 9 you will have to add 10 on the second time round for the display.

Extra components required: BCD counter IC (4510B); BCD decoder-driver (4511B); 7-segment LED display, common cathode; resistor – 220 Ω (red red brown).

2 *'Battleships'*. This well-known game can be played as a variation. You could make your 'battleships' occupy two locations in each memory address by storing data consisting of four-bit 'words' having two adjacent '1's, e.g. 1100 or 0110 or 0011. The attacker trying to sink your fleet would have to press two of *S*5, *S*6, *S*7 and *S*8 at the same time. Have a go.

8 Electronic adder

This circuit will add two decimal numbers and display the answer in decimal – so long as it is less than 10! But if you prefer the answer in binary, you can add up to 30 as explained in *Things to try* 3. There is no chance of it making your electronic calculator redundant but it does demonstrate very well the principles of electronic addition. You could call it a 'baby' digital computer.

WHAT YOU NEED

Keyboard encoder IC (74C922); two universal shift register ICs (4035B); full adder IC (4008B); BCD decoder-driver IC (4511B); 7-segment LED display; hexadecimal matrix keyboard; keyboard push switch; slide switch SPDT; LED; resistors – 220 Ω (red red brown), 680 Ω (blue grey brown), 100 kΩ (brown black yellow); ceramic capacitors – 0.01 µF, 0.1 µF; 9 V battery; battery clip connector; two circuit boards; PVC-covered tinned copper wire 1/0.6 mm.

HERE IS THE CIRCUIT

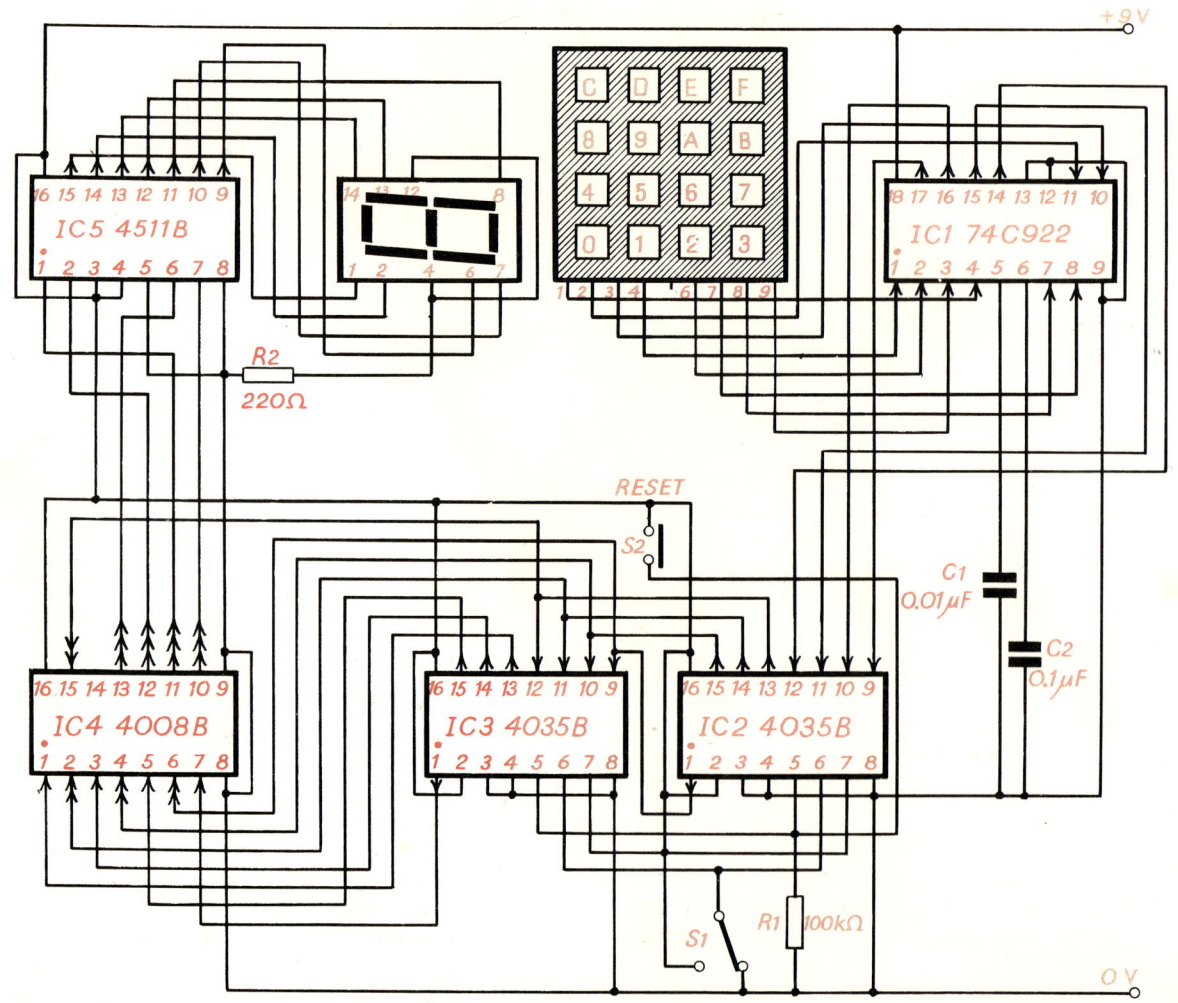

IC PIN CONNECTIONS: 74C922 (p.22), 4035B (p.16), 4008B (p.20), 4511B (p.22)
LED display (p.23 but see also p.63)

HOW TO BUILD IT

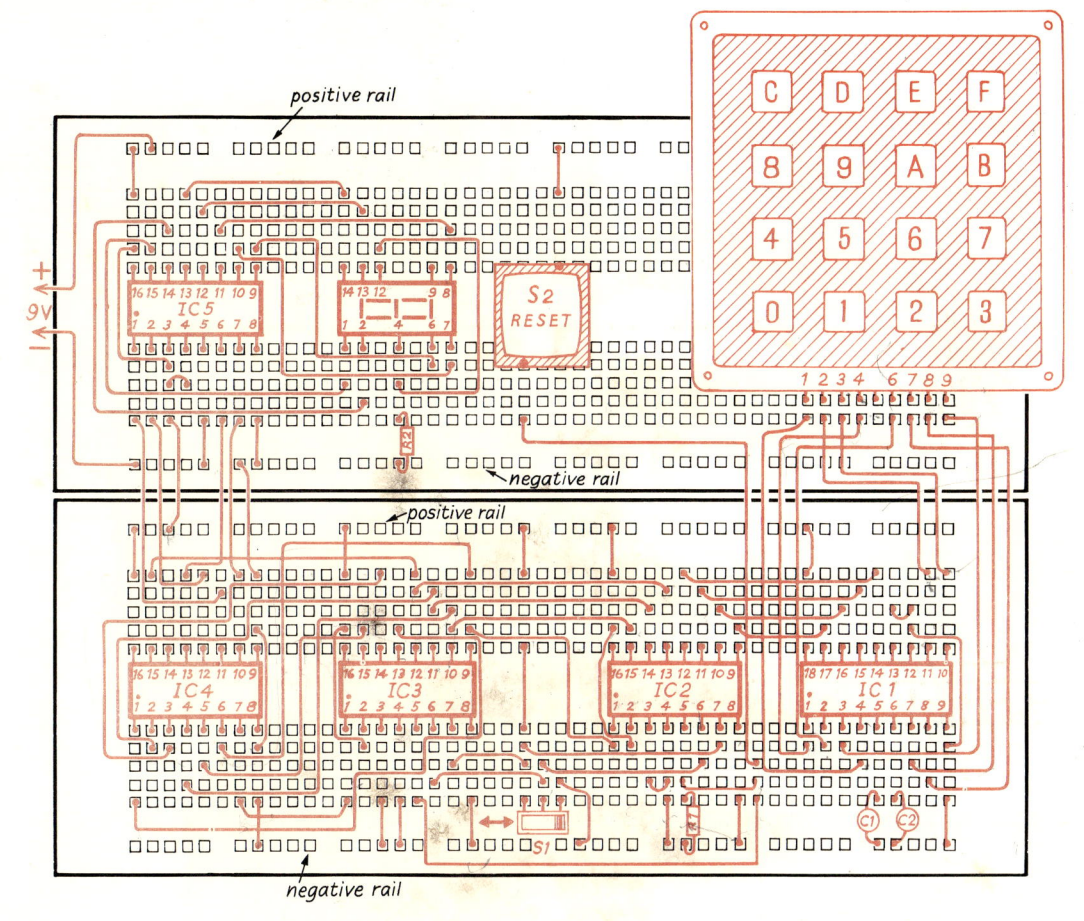

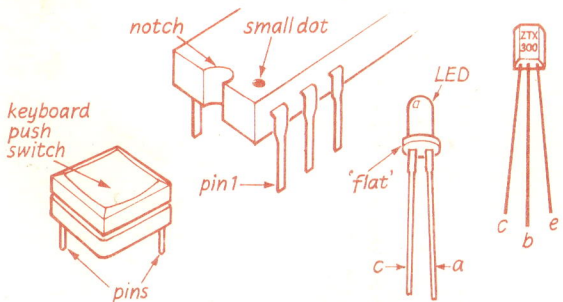

1. Couple two circuit boards together, side by side.
2. Identify pin 1 on the ICs from the small dot or notch at one end of the case. Carefully push each IC into the board in the position shown, taking care not to bend the pins. Also insert the 7-segment LED display.
3. Insert wire links from each IC to the positive and negative rails and between other sockets, as shown.
4. Insert $R1$, $R2$, $C1$, $C2$, $S1$, $S2$ and the matrix keyboard, taking great care with the latter to ensure that its 9 pins (only 8 of which are used) go into the correct sockets in the circuit board.
5. CHECK THE CIRCUIT CAREFULLY.
6. Connect the battery with the *correct polarity*. Ensure that $S1$ is switched to the right. Press $S2$ (the reset switch) if the number on the display is not '0' (or if it is not lit up). Now press say '3' on the keyboard. When $S1$ is pushed to the left and back to the right again, the '3' should appear on the display. Next press say '5' on the keyboard. This time when $S1$ is pushed left then right, the total of $5 + 3 = 8$ should appear on the display. Pressing $S2$ returns the display to '0' again.

Other 'sums' are suggested on page 61.

HOW IT WORKS

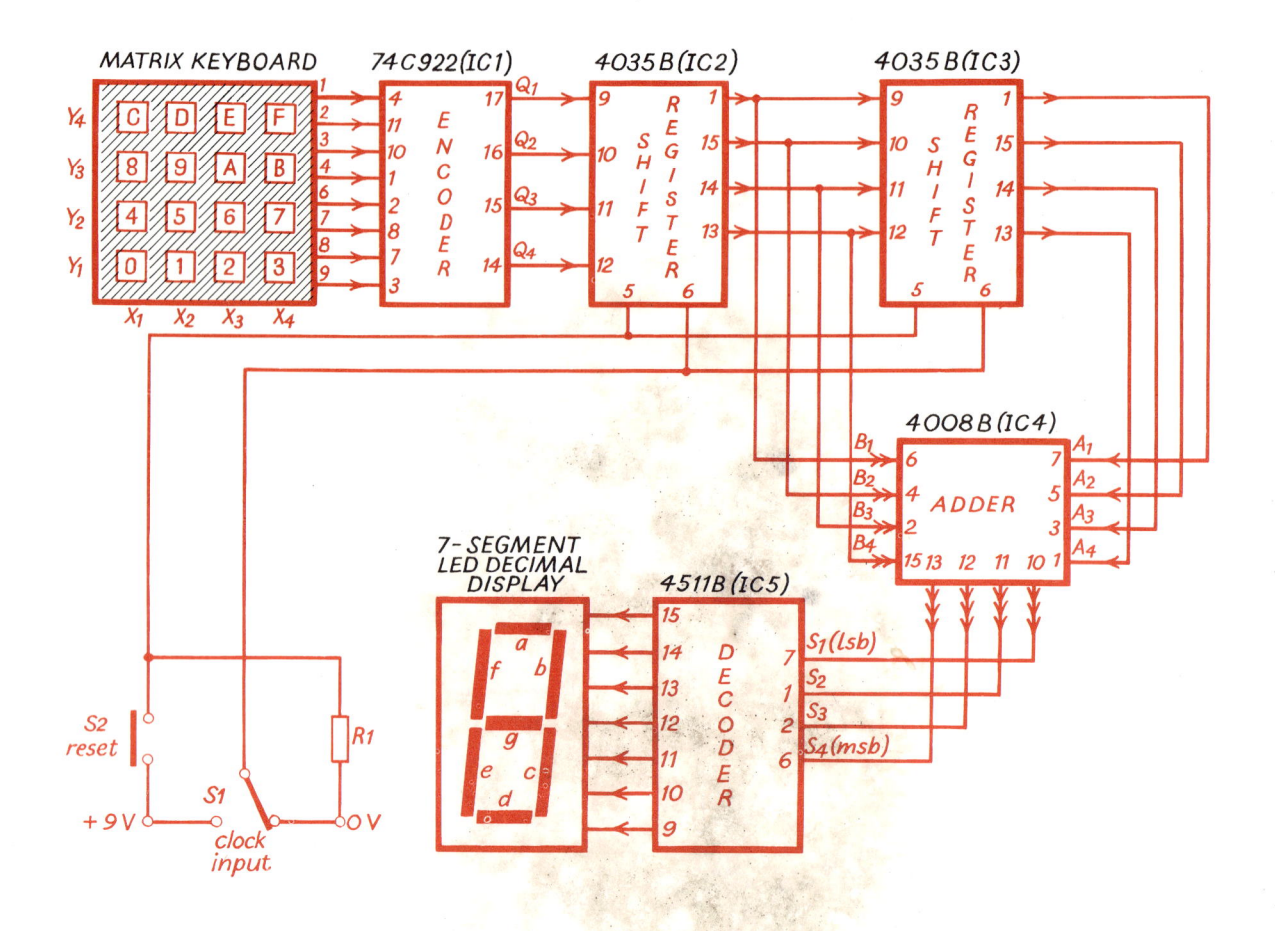

When a key is pressed on the MATRIX KEYBOARD, the four outputs Q_1, Q_2, Q_3 and Q_4 (pins 17, 16, 15 and 14) on the ENCODER go 'high' or 'low' as shown in the truth table below. A decimal number from 0 to 9 or a letter from A to F is converted into a four-bit binary number.

For example, if '3' is pressed, Q_1 and Q_2 go 'high' and Q_3 and Q_4 are 'low', i.e. the binary number applied from the outputs of the ENCODER to the inputs (pins 9, 10, 11 and 12) of the first SHIFT REGISTER (IC2) is 0011.

The 'clock inputs' (pin 6) on the SHIFT

Output	Key pressed															
	0 X_1Y_1	1 X_2Y_1	2 X_3Y_1	3 X_4Y_1	4 X_1Y_2	5 X_2Y_2	6 X_3Y_2	7 X_4Y_2	8 X_1Y_3	9 X_2Y_3	A(10) X_3Y_3	B(11) X_4Y_3	C(12) X_1Y_4	D(13) X_2Y_4	E(14) X_3Y_4	F(15) X_4Y_4
Q_1(lsb)	0	1	0	1	0	1	0	1	0	1	0	1	0	1	0	1
Q_2	0	0	1	1	0	0	1	1	0	0	1	1	0	0	1	1
Q_3	0	0	0	0	1	1	1	1	0	0	0	0	1	1	1	1
Q_4(msb)	0	0	0	0	0	0	0	0	1	1	1	1	1	1	1	1

REGISTERS are normally 'low' but when S1 is switched from 0 V to 9 V to 0 V, the resulting *rising edge* (⌐) causes the 'high' or 'low' states of the four inputs to be shifted to the outputs (pins 1, 15 14 and 13). The output states of the first SHIFT REGISTER are therefore $Q_1 = 1$, $Q_2 = 1$, $Q_3 = 0$ and $Q_4 = 0$. These become the inputs to the second SHIFT REGISTER (IC3).

If key '5' is now pressed, the binary number applied to the input of the first SHIFT REGISTER becomes 0101, i.e. $Q_1 = 1$, $Q_2 = 0$, $Q_3 = 1$ and $Q_4 = 0$. When S1 is switched as before to send a second clock pulse to the SHIFT REGISTERS, the first number (0011 = 3) is shifted from the input of the second SHIFT REGISTER to its outputs where it becomes the $A_4 A_3 A_2 A_1$ input (pins 1, 3, 5 and 7) to the ADDER (A_1 being the lsb and A_4 the msb). *At the same time* the second number (0101 = 5) is shifted from the inputs of the first SHIFT REGISTER to its outputs and becomes the $B_4 B_3 B_2 B_1$ input (pins 15, 2 4 and 6) to the ADDER.

The ADDER adds the two binary numbers $A_4 A_3 A_2 A_1$ and $B_4 B_3 B_2 B_1$ immediately and produces their binary sum $S_4 S_3 S_2 S_1$ at its outputs (pins 13, 12, 11 and 10). In this case the sum is 1000 (=8) so that $S_4 = 1$ and $S_3 = S_2 = S_1 = 0$. These outputs are applied to the four inputs (pins 6, 2, 1 and 7) of the DECODER which converts the binary number they represent into seven outputs a, b, c, d, e, f, g, each capable of driving directly one segment of the 7-SEGMENT LED DECIMAL DISPLAY. Here all seven outputs from the DECODER go 'high' causing all the segments to light up and give an '8' as the sum of 3 + 5.

'Reset' (pin 5) on the SHIFT REGISTERS is kept 'low' to load the registers – because of the connection to 0 V via R1. When switch S2 is pressed briefly, the 'resets' go 'high' and cause all inputs on both registers to go 'low'. The display then shows '0'.

THINGS TO TRY

1 *Hexadecimal code.* This code is also used in computers and covers all sixteen possibilities (0 to 15) of a four-bit binary code using either a single number or a letter. It consists of the ten decimal numbers 0 to 9 and first six letters of the alphabet, A to F, to represent 10 to 15.

A BCD decoder can handle only the numbers 0 to 9 and so if, after resetting the display to '0', you try to enter any of the letters from the hexadecimal keyboard, the display goes blank. Check this.

2 *Addition for totals between 16 and 25.* When the sum $S_4 S_3 S_2 S_1$ from the adder exceeds 15 (1111), the 'carry out' (pin 14) on it goes 'high'. If an LED is connected to 'carry out' as shown, it will light up if the sum of the two numbers being added is 16 or more.

To check this, start with the 7-segment display showing '0' (i.e. press S2), then following the same procedure as before, add '9' + '7'. The LED should light and the display remain at '0', indicating the total is 16, i.e. the five-bit number 10000. Repeat for '9' + '8'. The LED will again light up but the display goes to '1', giving a total of 16 + 1 = 17.

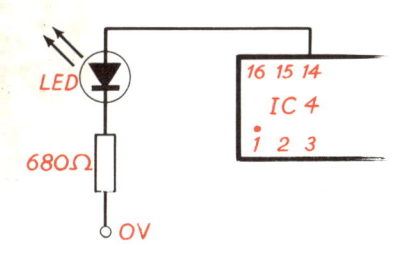

Now try adding A (=10) and B (=11). The total of 21 will be indicated by the LED being lit (16) and the display showing '5'.

Predict and then check what the number on the *display* will be when you add each of the following:

6 + A; 7 + B; D + 9; E + 5; A + C; C + D.

Remember to reset the display to '0' before each addition.

61

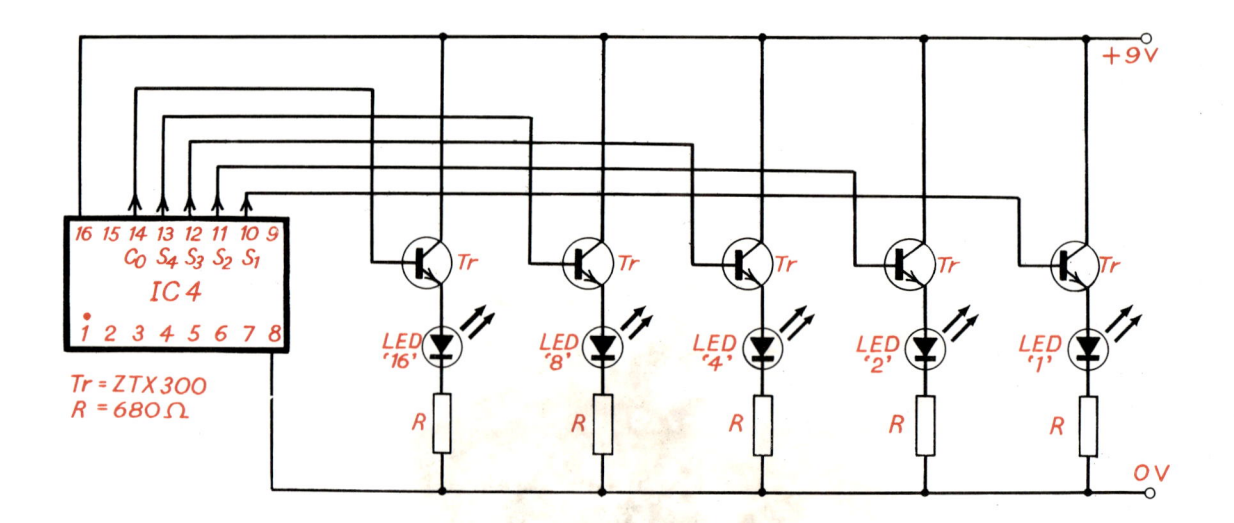

3 *Addition up to 30 with the answer in binary.* Change the output circuits from the adder as shown below so that C_0, S_4, S_3, S_2 and S_1 (pins 14, 13, 12, 11 and 10 respectively) each drive an LED via a transistor.

Press *S2* (reset) so that all five LEDs are off. Now enter *in turn*, '1', '2', '4', '8', and '8 + 8', into the adder by pressing the appropriate key(s) on the keyboard and resetting to zero between each entry. The corresponding LED should come on in each case, all others being off.

Add 15 (F) + 15 (F). All LEDs should be alight except that for '1', i.e. for the least significant bit, giving a total of 16 + 8 + 4 + 2 + 0 = 30.

PARTS LIST (COMPLETE)

- 2 circuit boards, e.g. *Bimboard, Experimentor 300, Balinu, Prototype* board, *ACE, Superstrip*, etc.
- 2 CMOS quad 2-input NOR gate ICs (4001B or 14001B)
- 1 CMOS dual 4-input NOR gate IC (4002B or 14002B)
- 1 CMOS quad 2-input NAND gate IC (4011B or 14011B)
- 1 dual astable/monostable IC (556)
- 1 CMOS astable/monostable IC (4047B)
- 1 CMOS dual D flip-flop IC (4013B or 14013B)
- 1 CMOS quad D latch IC (4042B or 14042B)
- 1 CMOS binary counter IC (4516B or 14516B)
- 1 CMOS BCD counter IC (4510B or 14510B)
- 1 CMOS decade counter IC (4017B or 14017B)
- 2 CMOS universal shift register ICs (4035B or 14035B)
- *1 CMOS 16-word 4-bit RAM IC (40114B)
- 1 CMOS full adder IC (4008B or 14008B)
- 1 CMOS magnitude comparator IC (4585B or 14585B)
- 1 CMOS BCD decoder-driver IC (4511B or 14511B)
- 1 CMOS keyboard encoder IC (74C922)
- 1 7-segment LED display, common cathode – *all do not have the same pin connections as those shown on page 23.*
- 5 npn transistors, e.g. ZTX300
- 10 LEDs (6 red, 2 yellow, 2 green) – *low current, high brightness types suitable for low current ICs.*
- 1 loudspeaker 2½ in (63 mm), 25 to 80 Ω
- 1 miniature p.c.b. slide switch SPDT
- 5 keyboard push switches (4 blue, 1 red)
- 2 d.i.l. 4-SPST switches
- 1 matrix keyboard (hexadecimal)
- 5 m PVC-covered tinned copper wire 1/0.6 mm
- 10 cm plastic sleeving 2 mm bore
- 50 cm plastic sleeving 1 mm bore
- 1 battery 9 V, e.g. PP3
- 1 battery clip connector
- 33 resistors, carbon ½ watt, 100 Ω, 220 Ω, six 680 Ω, 1 kΩ, 4.7 kΩ, three 10 kΩ, 27 kΩ, 47 kΩ, fourteen 100 kΩ, 220 kΩ, 470 kΩ, 1 MΩ, 2.2 MΩ
- 5 ceramic capacitors, three 0.01 μF, two 0.1 μF
- 3 electrolytic capacitors, two 1 μF, 4.7 μF

PARTS LIST ('ADD-ON')

The following items, when added to the *Adventures with Microelectronics* kit, will enable all the projects in *Adventures with Digital Electronics* to be built.

- 1 circuit board (see Parts list (complete))
- 2 CMOS quad 2-input NOR gate ICs (4001B or 14001B)
- 1 CMOS dual 4-input NOR gate IC (4002B or 14002B)
- 1 CMOS full adder IC (4008B or 14008B)
- 2 CMOS universal shift register ICs (4035B or 14035B)
- 1 CMOS quad D latch IC (4042B or 14042B)
- 1 CMOS magnitude comparator IC (4585B or 14585B)
- *1 CMOS 16-word 4-bit RAM IC (40114B)
- 1 CMOS keyboard encoder IC (74C922)
- 3 npn transistors, e.g. ZTX300
- 4 LEDs (2 red, 1 yellow, 1 green)
- 5 keyboard push switches (4 blue, 1 red)
- 2 d.i.l. 4-SPST switches
- 1 matrix keyboard (hexadecimal)
- 12 resistors, carbon, ½ watt, 100 kΩ
- 1 ceramic capacitor, 0.01 μF.

Items in the *Adventures with Microelectronics* kit which may require replacements are:

- 1 battery 9 V
- 1 battery clip connector
- 5 m PVC-covered tinned copper wire 1/0.6 mm
- 10 cm plastic sleeving 2 mm bore

* See *Addresses*, page 64.

ADDRESSES

A kit of good quality parts for *Adventures with Digital Electronics* can be bought from:

Unilab Ltd, Clarendon Road, Blackburn, Lancs, BB1 9TA. *Tel.* 0254 57643.

They also supply the *Adventures with Microelectronics* kit.

Many firms supplying electronic components advertise in *Everyday Electronics*, *Practical Wireless* and other magazines.

Note. Components advertised as 'manufacturer's surplus', 'near equivalent to' or 'untested' are often rejects sold cheaply because they are substandard. This applies especially to integrated circuits, LEDs and transistors. Reputable firms generally publish catalogues.

If you have a local electronics shop you may find it convenient to get components there.

Schools and colleges can obtain supplies from:

RS Components Ltd, P.O. Box 99, Corby, Northants, NN17 9RS (catalogue free).

Manufacturers making the various circuit boards are:

Bimboard: Boss Industrial Mouldings Ltd, 2 Herne Hill Road, London SE24 0AU.

Experimentor 300: Continental Specialties Corporation (UK) Ltd, Shire Hill Industrial Estate, Saffron Walden, Essex, CB11 3AQ.

ACE and Superstrip: Letrokit Ltd, Sutton Industrial Park, London Road, Earley, Reading, Berks, RG6 1AZ.

★The CMOS 40114B (16-word 4-bit RAM IC) can be obtained from:

Access Electronics Components, Jubilee House, Jubilee Road, Letchworth, Herts, SG6 1QH.
Tel. 04626 2333